The Shameless Plug:

"The Curse of my Father"

Written By:

Taunishia Zoa

Copyright

The Shameless Plug: "The Curse of my Father"

Table of Contents

Dedication

To you, Patricia Faye Epps, with tears in my eyes, I dedicate this memoir. I personally just wish Heaven had a phone so that I could thank you one last time. I mean, thank you for everything. While you were on this earth, I did not feel like I thanked you enough. You are, by far, the strongest woman I will ever know. I see you as an amazing mother, an impeccable wife, a mentor, a confidante, a prayer warrior, a nurturer, an encourager, and the list goes on. You made detrimental sacrifices for us without thinking twice. You were the epitome of grace and selflessness. There are literally not enough words in the dictionary to honor a woman of your caliber. There will never be another soul like you. It is crazy how all the wisdom you gave me while you were alive seemed in vain. I just want to let you know that I absorbed it all, even when you thought I wasn't listening. I miss you so much, mom, and though I have made a thousand mistakes, when the thought of me giving up reigns, I hear your voice pushing me through it all.

I have four little boys now. You would have loved all of them. Cameron is blossoming into a little man. He is so smart, and he spent the most time with you, so he remembers you. Sometimes he randomly asks me about you, and he smiles at all my responses. According to the stories you used to tell, he resembles me in so many ways with being talented, witty, ingenious, and exuding stubbornness. What a combo!

Some days he cries for you. It is hard to even digest watching him weep over the bond that you two shared in a short amount of time. That just shows the impact you had on not only him but to everyone you encountered.

Connor is my second oldest, and he is clearly going to preach the word one day. But mom, his heart is so pure, and he really loves God at the tender young age of three! I am not sure when he first heard God's voice, but it could have possibly been around the age of two years old when he kept me from getting a speeding ticket while driving without a license!

Channing is the knee baby, and he is a spectacular kid as well. He is deeply passionate about everything down to his toy trucks and music. Channing is also the lover, and his timing is always perfect with his hugs and kisses. He reminds me of you a lot when I look into his eyes.

The baby's name is Colin! Although I am still learning his personality daily, I know that he is always on the go! I bet you are in Heaven laughing out loud because I can hear you saying, "He got that honest!"

Mom, I just wanted to let you know that I am going to protect these babies with every fiber of my being. I recollect you being concerned about me being a mother because of my selfishness. I think I was more concerned than you were at the time. But losing you made me realize a plethora of things. Not only did I need to implement your wisdom, but I also needed to become the woman you always knew I could be, and needed to develop my own relationship with God because I no longer had you to intercede on my behalf.

The great news is, I am figuring this thing out one day at a time, a process I will never refute.

Some days I feel your presence, and I silently cry tears of joy. I hope it's not too selfish of me to ask you to continue to watch over us and show up in those moments when there's a lag in my response regarding how I am raising boys that will one day become men.

I promise I am going to make you proud!

I love you. Forever and a day.

Acknowledgements

First and foremost, I would like to acknowledge my four wonderful, handsome boys for inspiring me to be better and pursue my dreams of being an author. You four literally changed my life. I know that times were not always easy for us, but I made sacrifices to make sure you guys had everything you ever needed. I know there were critical moments and times I cannot get back, but I have prayed prayers over you guys to cover you from being affiliated with any orphan spirits. You guys mean the world to me, and you literally saved my life. It is because of you that I look forward to a new day daily. Thank you, guys, for being the best kids in the world.

I would like to express my gratitude to the many people who saw me through this book; to all those who provided support, talked things over with me, read excerpts, shared wisdom, allowed me to quote their remarks and assisted in the editing, prophesied and/or spoke into my life and contributed to proofreading and design.

I would like to thank my best friends, Jennifer Mason and Samara Scott for believing in me to get my book done. I know it was a long and difficult journey for them, and I could never repay you guys for listening to me vent, cry, be worried, discouraged, and all the above. You, ladies, are MY ROCK!

I would like to thank Norah Sarsour by way of California for walking me through this process and taking up time with me that was allotted possibly for prior engagements. In addition, I know she sacrificed time spent with her beautiful daughter in helping me in the process of selection and editing a percentage of my book.

Sentiments to Rob McKiver (CEO of The Gent's Life) for his vision in bringing my apparel line to life, encouraging me to keep pushing towards my goals, dreams and inspiration and being my personal therapist on those cumbersome days. You're the first person that identified my demons and made sure they were inescapable so I could face them head on. "How long will you utilize your past rejection as an excuse?" I can recollect you asking me while I sat in silence. In addition, thank you for allowing me to be myself in a judgment free, safe zone. Love you GT.

Thank you and acknowledgements to Jason Tyree, who designed my book cover. He was able to embrace my vision and nailed it on the first time.

Last and not least: "I beg forgiveness of all those who have been with me over the course of the years and whose names I have failed to mention.

Please charge it to my mind and not my heart.

Preface

While journaling as my mother transitioned out of this world back in 2012, I found myself with an array of emotions very often, and the only way I could express myself was to write. Being vulnerable is something that I have struggled with my entire life. Therefore, journaling my emotions and thoughts on paper became my vice.

I decided to write this book in its entirety merely to share my story. At a young age, I endured a lot. The most prominent memory that stood out to me was not having my biological father in my life. Fathers carry identity associated with their children. A chunk of who I was simply was missing, and the struggle of my life of being without a father was heightened as I wrote my memories in before I also lost my mother. I started to write to search for a guide; if I had lived this much without my biological father, then perhaps I had it in me to somehow survive the loss of my mother.

I realized that as my mother began her exit from this world, the thoughts I had are those that have persisted through various intervals of my life. It is an interesting thing to write out memories and look for your own truths in that writing. But at the same time, I kept telling myself that the past was only on paper now, in this book, and that it would not limit me to the covers. Rather than define me, this series is a blueprint to my personalized survival guide, with every mistake and moment of rawness there. I want the little girl, the single parent, or the woman who has resentment towards their absentee father to understand the significance of decisions made from the past, when we have the ability to author our future.

My memoir pulls you into scenes of my life. The chapters speak to my identity that grows in place of the void left by my father: the unpopular kid at school, the kid who was attention seeking but was shunned by peers, the adult who struggled with promiscuity and sexuality, the woman who equated love with gifts and money, manipulating the power of sex to thrive, the woman who becomes the enemy to her significant other because she opts to not have an abortion, the woman who comes face-to-face with death, the woman who became a single mother.

My journey in writing this memoir kicked up the dust of unsettled trauma. I felt broken most days as I wrote this book. I can honestly say that writing this book has significantly changed who I am. Now I am more apologetic and cognizant of my actions not only for myself, but for strangers, my audience, anyone that may look up to me, my kids, friends and family and everyone that loves me.

Trials and tribulations with any projects or passions is the inevitable. I went through three different editors while completing this book. I also had graphic designers that took my money and did not respond once they realized that my vision was potentially too immense for their liking. I learned that as a babe in this author game, you have to give yourself realistic timelines, focus, be vigilant, and actually commit to "doing the work." I have learned to be okay with not wanting to be associated with mediocrity in regard to anything that my name is attached to. When these challenges presented themselves, I opted for an alternative route and continued on my journey. By definition, a journey is considered an act of traveling from one place to another. I have realized that everyone's journey won't resemble yours. We eventually have to find our own way, and mine has taken a little over *seven* years now. There were days I would be angry that I endured certain things in those settings, and I would put the laptop away and wouldn't touch it for days, sometimes even months because it hurt to be in "that place" once again.

Moses and the Israelites were in the wilderness for forty years due to disobedience. You do not have to wander forty years to do what God called you to do. It's never, ever too late to start that business, write that book, become a parent, get married, or find peace.

Chapter 1: Misfit Matters

I was born into a family of two boys who became my older brothers, which made me the youngest of three children. My biological father and my mother first met in 1973. My father was twenty years old and stood five-feet-eleven with very dark skin. His eyes were a glassy dark-blue. Women said that my dad had bedroom eyes.

My mother was a tender sixteen years of age and still a virgin. She was an exotic bi-racial mix of Caucasian and African American to depict her high-yellow tone. She was, for sure, a redbone with sandy-red hair hanging past her buttocks. In addition, her teeth were perfectly white, and she had a face full of red and brownish freckles. My mother was shaped like a Coca-Cola bottle with curves for days. Because of the way she looked and matured physically, my grandmother kept her in the house for the majority of the time. She was only allowed out of the house to go to school and back. She was also the primary caregiver for her six-year-old brother while my grandmother ran the streets, hustling and operating the local liquor houses. My grandmother was super -

strict and did not play when it came to boys or men talking to her daughter; she practically scared everyone off. Everyone in the neighborhood knew my grandmother carried a gun and she was not afraid to use it. However, that did not stop my father from pursuing her; my grandmother was unaware that she was about to meet her match.

My mother stepped off the school bus one day coming from Hillside High School when she noticed a maroon Camaro pass by. She began the half-mile walk home in the opposite direction when she heard screeching tires and the smooth hum of the Camaro's engine approach from behind.

"Gorgeous," he said as he rode beside her slowly.

My mother remained silent and picked up her pace. Although she was used to men pursuing her, this pursuit seemed a bit more aggressive than others.

"What's a man like me need to do to take a beautiful young lady like yourself out on a date?" he asked.

"My mother doesn't let me talk to boys," she responded.

"That's even better because I'm not a boy, I am a grown man," he said.

My mother's reality meant there was no way she could even entertain this chocolate man, especially knowing how her mother would react if she found out. So, she veered off to the green house and walked in the door without looking back.

My father stopped his car in front of the green house and smiled. He knew where my mother stayed now. There was no hiding from him.

The next morning, my mother returned to her normal routine of getting herself ready for school first, then getting her younger brother dressed for school, and out the door thirty minutes early. My mother was in complete shock as she approached the school bus and saw the same maroon Camaro from the day before. The Camaro's driver-side door swung open.

"Well, good morning, gorgeous!" my father said to her.

"You know you're going to get me in trouble, right? My mother is crazy, and there is no way she would ever let me see you! So please, go away!" my mother pleaded.

"Well, guess what? I'm crazy too! Crazy is in my bloodline, and I respect my elders, but your mother is the least of my worries," he responded.

As scared as she was, this intrigued my mother, which caused her to let her guard down. With great caution, she engaged in small talk with him, sneaking in peeks at his Camaro and the chunky gold chains around his neck. She wondered what he did for a living.

The bus arrived, and my mother quickly boarded it.

"I'll see you around," my father called out.

Days of these bus stop meetings turned into months. My father became frustrated because he didn't even have her phone number yet, not from the lack of trying. Every time he asked, she instantly shut him down. Unbeknownst to him, my mother was falling for my father daily. The thirty-minute departure times from home to the bus stop had turned into her leaving an hour early so that she could spend time with him. One evening, my father did not show up at the bus stop, and my mother stood there waiting. That was out of his routine, and she wondered where he was. After thirty minutes of waiting, she made her way to the green house and found my grandmother sitting on the front porch.

"Why are you so late coming from the bus stop?" she asked sternly.

My mother instantly tensed up and wondered if someone had snitched on her long meetings with my father after school.

"I missed the school bus, so I had to take the city bus home," she stuttered.

My grandmother's eyes narrowed as she puffed on her cigarette. Afraid of what my grandmother might know, my mother put her things down in her bedroom, gathered herself, and hurried back onto the front porch to join her mother for a temperature check.

"How was your day, mom?" she asked.

"Why are you so nervous and acting sneaky? Get out of my face!" she said, motioning my mother to get out of her view of passing cars.

As my mother began to feel relieved that my grandmother had no clue about the clandestine bus stop meetings, she heard an engine roar.

She looked at my grandmother in feigned confusion as the Camaro slowly pulled up to the front of the green house and parked. The engine roared as my mother and grandmother exchanged looks.

The car windows of the Camaro were tinted black, and from the distance of the porch, you would not know who was in it unless *YOU* knew who was in it.

"Who is that, baby doll?" my grandmother asked.

My mother shrugged as the Camaro sped off into the night.

She went to her room to lay down across her bed and worried about what types of tricks my father had up his sleeve. Still, it warmed her heart to be pursued by a man. That night, she laid in bed and smiled at the thought of him as she drifted off to sleep.

The following weeks came and went with no sign of my father. Maybe he lost interest, since he had to go through my grandmother even to get access to her. One day after school, my mother heard the familiar roaring engine outside of the house, and she ran to look out the window.

"He came back," she whispered to herself.

This time, my father parked his car in the driveway and walked up to the door.

My mother paced around her room, overwhelmed with anxiety. What did he want? What was he going to say to my grandmother? No way could this be a good turnout.

The doorbell rang loudly, and for my mother, it seemed like it had been ringing for an eternity. She cracked her door open to hear the dialogue.

"Is Terri home?" my father asked before briefly clearing his throat.

My grandmother stared him up and down and said, "Who are you?"

"Ma'am, with all due respect, my name is Don Rogers," he said politely.

"What business do you have with Terri?" my grandmother asked sternly.

"Ma'am, I think your daughter is gorgeous, and I have spoken to her in passing on occasion. So, if you do not mind, with your blessing, I would like the opportunity to chat with her for a few minutes," my father replied.

My grandmother stood there in disbelief that my father dared to knock on her front door. She looked out at his car and back at him before opening the screen door.

My grandmother knew money when she saw it.

"You have five minutes," she told him as she backed away from the door, still sizing him up.

"Terri! There's some man out here to see you, and you better make it quick," my grandmother said.

My mother came out of the room with feelings of extreme nervousness and excitement wrapped together.

"What are you doing here?" she said quietly with her eyes as big as two fifty-cent pieces.

"I came to see you. Your mother said I only have five minutes, so is it okay if I call you sometime?" he asked, smiling from ear-to-ear.

"Sure," my mother said with her hands tucked in her back pocket.

She gave my father the landline number to the house.

He kissed her on the forehead before backing out the front door with the phone number tucked in his hand.

That was the start of something beautiful, according to all parties involved. My mother could not believe that my grandmother had let him in to even talk to her. But my grandmother was all about her money, and she knew my father had it. She recognized a potential benefit when she saw one.

By knocking on my grandmother's front door, my father broke sacred ground and opened the door for chaos to reign.

Months of daily phone calls and increasingly extended visits to the house emboldened my grandmother to step out for errands while my father stayed behind with my mother and her younger brother.

That's when the sex started. My mother had finally lost her virginity, and she was head-over-heels in love with my pops.

Soon after, my father called on a Saturday to get permission to come by and take her out for the weekend, but he was told that my mother was not home. My grandmother did not sound like her usual self; she was short with my father.

"Terri is not home! She's at the clinic!" she said forcefully.

"The clinic? Which one? I need to get there now!" he asked.

"She's at Lincoln, if you must know," she mumbled before hanging up,

My father rushed down to the clinic, where he blazed a path, asking for my mother until someone was able to point him in the right direction.

"Sir, she's in the recovery area in the back of the building," the receptionist informed my father.

My father rushed back to where my mother lay. Her face was flushed.

"Terri, are you okay?" my father asked.

My mother's eyes got big as two quarters when she saw my father push those curtains back. She was four months pregnant and hadn't told my father about the baby because she never had a chance. By the time she figured out what was going on with her body, my grandmother had figured it out and made her terminate the pregnancy.

"Oh, Don, they were twins!" she cried.

"What do mean, Terri?" he asked in confusion.

"I found out I was pregnant with twins, and my mother made me come here to have an abortion!" she cried.

My father felt anger raging as he held my mother while she cried out to him.

"That's okay! You will get pregnant again, and this time we will run away," he said.

That seemed to console my mother.

My father helped my mother get dressed and took her home. He was so pissed; he couldn't stick around or look my grandmother in the face.

"I love you, and I'll see you later," he told my mother.

The next morning my mother started off to school, and my father was at the bus stop waiting on her.

"Get in," he said.

"What about school?" my mother asked.

"Do you want to be with me or not?"

"Of course, I do," she said, rubbing his head.

"Run away with me. I want you to marry me, Terri!" he told her.

"Are you serious?" she asked with a burst of excitement.

"Yes, we will stay at my mother's for a while and then head to South Carolina to get hitched," he said.

My mother was down with the plan, and she buckled her seat belt as they rode off. They laid low at my father's mother's house for a month before they got the news that my grandmother had put an APB out for them.

"We can't stay here. We've got to go now!" my father said.

They headed to South Carolina, where my father grew up and had family. They were intimate during that month, and then my mother's period was late. My father didn't want to get his own place because of the inevitable paper trail left in his wake. Plus, my mother was probably pregnant again, and if the baby were going to be born there, they would need help.

My mother visited a doctor who confirmed she was pregnant again. They were super-elated to start their own family, and they needed to get married ASAP.

They went to the local courthouse and got hitched the next morning. My mother was happy that she was finally going to be with my father for the rest of her life, but her heart and mind were still in North Carolina. She missed her little brother something crazy, and some nights, she cried profusely in my father's arms.

My father wanted to do anything to make sure my mother did not stress while carrying their second baby. Besides, doctors always advise you to heal after a miscarriage or abortion before getting pregnant again. Even though they were wanted in the state of North Carolina, he made plans to get her back there, so she could see her little brother.

At this point, my grandmother was not aware of the second baby that was soon to be born into the world, and my father wanted to keep it that way. He planned to stay gone, if possible, to ensure that no doctor would touch her. The goal was to return to North Carolina when she was about seven months pregnant.

In the meantime, my father and mother would sneak back into North Carolina for no more than twenty-four hours to see my father's mother and my mother's little brother. She would sneak to the playground while he was at school, and he used to beg and cry to go with her. She assured him he couldn't go with her at that time, but she would be back soon. It was obvious that my mother was pregnant at the time, but she made her little brother promise not to tell my grandmother that he had seen her and that she was pregnant.

Her little brother assured her that their secret was safe with him, and he would return to the playground with the other kids watching the Camaro drive away until it was no longer in sight. After dodging the police on multiple occasions when they were tipped off about my parent's whereabouts, my mother had finally reached her seven-month mark in her pregnancy. It was time to return to North Carolina so that she could deliver the baby there.

My mother was now a married woman and expecting a new baby, but that fear of what her mother would do or say still played in the back of her mind. That was the longest four-hour trip for my mother driving from South Carolina back to North Carolina. After they arrived, they rested at my father's mother's house and enjoyed all the positive vibes about my mother expecting her firstborn.

The next morning, they headed out to tell my grandmother the news. There was silence as they pulled up to the green house. My father cut the engine, and they sat in the car motionless.

"Are you ready?" he asked my mother in his softest tone.

"Of course! I mean, I am a married woman at this point. What's the worst she could do? Not talk to me anymore?" My mother unbuckled her seatbelt and wobbled up the paved driveway to the front door, while my father stayed in the car.

The screen door was locked as always, and my mother proceeded to knock.

No answer.

"Mama! Are you in here?" my mother called out.

It took a while for my grandmother to come to the door, and when she did, she just stared at my mother and her baby bump with disgust.

"I see you went and got yourself pregnant again, huh? Well, I hope he plans on marrying you because I'm not taking care of any babies!" my grandmother said.

"Mama, he *did* marry me. I'm married, Mama!" she exclaimed.

There was an awkward silence as my grandmother looked over the porch at my father sitting in the car. She finally unlocked the screen door and motioned for them to come in.

"Might as well come in here and get off your feet. I've had everybody looking for you!" my grandmother explained.

"Mama, I'm sorry about my actions, but I knew you would never allow me to keep this baby while staying under your roof," she said.

"What's done is done!" She turned to my father and said, "You better take care of my daughter!"

"Yes, ma'am," my father replied.

One of my grandmother's concerns was my mother popping up pregnant, which is why she kept her so guarded her entire life. Now, she was married to a drug dealer, so the concerns were all valid. What would happen if my father was arrested for selling drugs? That would force my mother into single motherhood, just like my grandmother.

My brother was born a preemie on the 9th of April in Durham, North Carolina. My parents were able to secure a house on the same block as my grandmother with some assistance from welfare. The house was a two-bedroom, two-floor duplex. It was not in the best neighborhood, but it was feasible for the time being. Because my father was still in the streets and hustling, my mother gave my brother her maiden name to secure assistance for housing, food, healthcare, etc.

As they got settled, my pops got back on the streets to find some "work," especially since he had depleted his savings bouncing state-to-state while they were on the run. Ideally, my mother wanted him to get a *real job* working for a company that had benefits. He assured her that was his goal, but she soon realized he was back on the streets selling drugs. She could tell because he started hanging out all times of the night. In addition, when he did get in, she would go through his pant pockets while he was sleeping and find products and piles of money.

My brother was having respiratory complications when he was first born and stayed in the hospital, so my mother couldn't work.

At two months, my brother was released to go home. The doctors said my mother would always need to monitor his breathing closely. One evening, while my mother was preparing dinner, she placed the pots on low heat to run upstairs and check on my brother. Lately, he'd been sleeping longer than his normal two-hour naps. As soon as my mother entered the room, she knew he was not breathing. As a new mom, she panicked. She swaddled my brother into his blue blanket, picked him up, and ran out of the house to Mrs. Anna's house across the street.

Mrs. Anna was the praying saint on the block, and my mother knew she could get a prayer through. Occasionally, they would speak in passing, and my mother was aware that she had a relationship with God. My mother banged on Mrs. Anna's door with her lifeless baby in her hands.

Mrs. Anna appeared at the door in her night robe and bonnet.

"What is it, my child? You are knocking like you're the police!" she said with her distinct raspy voice.

"Mrs. Anna! Please pray for my baby! He's not breathing!" my mother screamed.

Mrs. Anna instantly went into prayer warrior mode. She disappeared from the living room for a split second and returned with a tube of oil. Mrs. Anna proceeded to rub the oil on my brother's forehead and chest, and she started speaking in her heavenly language. In the meantime, one of the neighbors heard my mother's cries and screaming and called 911. After seven minutes of Mrs. Anna laying hands and praying, just as my mother opened the door for the paramedics, my brother started coughing and crying at the top of his lungs. The paramedics advised that he still needed to be taken to the hospital to be examined.

Upon arrival at the hospital, my mother held onto my brother as if that were the last time she was going to see him. Examinations and tests didn't reveal anything was wrong. The doctor's initial theory was he went into cardiac arrest because of his respiratory issues. However, these new results revealed the respiratory problems had vanished, and my brother had a clean bill of health. The doctors were literally scratching their heads because they recollected numerous hospital admissions within the last two months surrounding my brother's health. But at that moment, not a single trace of any abnormal blood work or breathing was apparent to these medical experts.

My mother learned early that her faith should never be in science and/or what man says. Even though she was not a devout Christian at the time, she knew of God, and this was a moment that she would never forget.

After surviving being a preemie and respiratory issues, my brother was literally a miracle baby!

While my mother relished in the mercy of the Lord, a darker force loomed in the house. She started noticing strange behavior in my pops. My father paced the house in the wee hours of the morning while talking to his dead father. Sometimes wives overlook red-flag behaviors for fear of being alone or having to raise kids by themselves, so she ignored it. However, it was evident that my father started getting high off his own supply. With crack-cocaine being the "it" thing in the 1980s that hit the street, my father got hooked on it himself.

Shortly after, he was arrested with drugs in his car and caught a two-year sentence, leaving my mother to fend for herself with my oldest brother.

During marital troubles, an immense amount of arguments, and my father constantly being in and out of prison, my mother popped up pregnant again with the knee baby. Although my mother knew her marriage was on the rocks, she carried my second brother to full term. However, she decided that she would get her tubes tied after giving birth to him. My mother was determined to get off public assistance, by finishing her GED, attending community college, and getting a job that would enable her to stand on her own two feet. She couldn't achieve that by bringing more kids into this unhealthy situation.

My mother made the mistake of relying on my father as transportation for the tubal ligation procedure. He was nowhere to be found on the day of her appointment, so she missed it.

My mother searched for work while my uncle assisted her with childcare. My uncle was practically a kid himself. The next four years were full of struggles to make ends meet. Choices between keeping the lights on, purchasing a new pair of shoes for herself or for us kids became the norm. Sometimes, there was *no* choice. My mother could not understand where my pop's money was going, especially since he left the house at noon and did not return until nightfall. He slept in every day, woke up in an ill mood, and then left the house without saying a word to anyone, including my brothers. My mother soon realized that he had to support his recently-acquired, astronomically-expensive drug habit.

Around the same time every evening, the house settled into a peaceful silence, with everyone sound asleep. Then, my father obliterated my mother's hard-won sanctity by tearing through the house, high out his mind, and, like an animal, tugged and pulled on her nightgown for sexual favors. My mother was unaware of what he was doing in those streets all day with other women, so she refused to have sex with him. This only fueled his fire, so my father ripped off her clothes and forced himself onto her until he was pleased. Then he would roll over and pass out with his pants around his ankles. I recollect the knee baby telling me a story (when we grew older) about how he was woken up out of his sleep by gunshots. My mother shot at my father in the bedroom because she was done with all of it – the rape, his absence, and the financial struggle. He was very blessed that my mother's aim was off as he ran off to take cover.

After that night, if my father came home at all, it was once or twice a week, and then he slept on the couch in the living room. He knew to stay clear of my mother's path.

My mother wanted a way out of the marriage but feared that she would never get out of the hood if she asked him to leave. The little income she had would come from my pops drug money and returning home to my grandmother's *I told you so* was not an option. Besides, she did not want her sons to grow up without a father. But as the days grew longer when he was around, she thought maybe it was wiser that her kids were not in such a toxic situation. She spent days pondering on better and how she could obtain it for herself and her two little boys at the time.

She was planning to put my pops out of the house. In the interim, she scheduled to have her tubes tied again since she missed the first appointment previously. She did not want any more kids coming into this situation with all the chaos. My mother continued to endure but started writing down an exit plan to leave my father.

My mother arrived at the clinic an hour early to get her tubes tied. She was putting an end to this situation once and for all. She had her mind made up; tying up her tubes meant severing any future with my pops.

The doctor prepared her for an outpatient procedure, and they started the preliminary testing. My mother was undressed and waiting for the procedure to start when they came back in and asked her to put her clothes back on.

"Is there something wrong, doctor? Why are you asking me to get dressed? I know doctors don't like to tie tubes on women this young, but I must get this done," she said.

My mother was ready to take on this new path away from my father, and then she realized the doctors discovered this distressing news. Was this discovery the Lord's way of saying maybe you should not take this path just yet?

"Well, in that case, Mrs. Edwards, I regret to inform you that you are with child," he said with a blank face.

With all that my mother had been through, from sneaking away and leaving her family behind, to dealing with her husband's absence, drug habits, numerous prison sentences, and violence, wasn't that enough? This news traumatized her.

As the clear path to freedom began to disintegrate, she struggled to piece together words.

"What do you mean?" she whispered, as the color flushed from her face.

Her downcast eyes should have pointed upward in her time of weakness, but who could judge a woman weary of being called, *that single mother*?

The thoughts raged like waves now, crashing back from ideas that had evaporated, and the rage built a loud tremble in her voice.

"This cannot be happening! I am in the process of leaving my husband!" she cried to the doctor, who offered no remedy to treat her prescribed destiny.

As she dressed and gathered her things, she could only run to the one who had planted this seed. But my father was not there. He was probably out with the mistress my mother recently found out about from my grandmother. One of her liquor store clients told my grandmother that my father's mistress was pregnant.

Chapter 2: Fathering Resentment

Dressed in the same clothes from four days before when he left with complete disregard, he returned unchanged, in clothes and attitude. My mother presented him with his belongings already packed up for him to carry off and leave this home. Twenty-nine years old with three kids and a deadbeat husband, she figured having the third without him would be easier than trying to factor him into an equation he wanted no part of. And so, she mentioned to him that they were expecting another child. However, his services as a husband were no longer needed.

In the interim, my mother found out later that my dad went to reside with the lady that showed up on my mother's doorstep, saying she was pregnant. Months went by of him not calling and not checking on his children. That was the new standard.

But then one day, there was a knock at the door.

It was my pops standing there looking dirty, skinny, and frantic, begging to come back home.

41

My mother invited my father in because that was the right thing to do since she was so forgiving, and they were still legally married. Even if he betrayed their vows, she honored hers virtuously.

My father had missed several doctors' appointments, and my mother had already found out she was having another boy. That day was very emotional for her because even though she did not want any more kids, she was hoping for a girl.

"So, the young lady that you're expecting a child with, what's your status?" she asked.

He looked up at her and replied softly, "I told her that I missed my family, and I wanted to be back with you guys. So, she said that if I left, I couldn't see my daughter, and she would make good on that."

"But that child is your family. I heard she is having a girl. Well, just in case you were wondering, we are expecting another boy," my mother faintly responded.

My pops dropped his head into his hands, feeling the wrath of all his mistakes. He assured my mother he was going to change; he just needed us.

My mother wanted to take him back, but all she could do was replay the day in her head when his mistress showed up in their yard, claiming to be pregnant with my father's child.

A cab pulled to the house, and a lady hopped out and wobbled to the backyard where my father and mother were pulling down laundry from the clothesline.

"Don? When you get a chance, I need you to come by the house; my aunt passed away," the lady said.

My mother had no idea what that verbiage meant. Besides, the lady never said one word to my mother; her eyes fixated on my father. According to this lady's body language, my mother saw that she was remarkably familiar with my father. Women *know*.

My mother looked the lady up and down, head-to-toe while holding a damp t-shirt. She looked over at my father as he shrugged. He never reacted to the distraught lady, who then disappeared back into the cab.

My mother watched the cab pull away, she looked over at my father one last time, dropped the wet t-shirt into the basket, and walked into the house.

She never said a word. My mother exuded resilience, and at this point, she was tired. She resembled the lady that popped up at the house because their bellies measured the same at first glance. She was about to have her third baby any day now, and she was so drained that she didn't have the energy to ask. She was more focused on having a healthy and safe delivery, so she retreated. For now.

Chapter 3: Meet your Maker

I was positioned in a certain way, that I wanted to start the year off full of surprises. I was hiding an identity that would dominate the rest of my life. I initially was scheduled to come late January, but the good Lord had other plans.

"Wake up! I need you to take me to the emergency room. My water just broke!" my mother yelled.

My mom was literally in labor with me for almost seventy-two hours. She was in so much pain, and the doctors encouraged her to have a cesarean with me, but she refused. She labored and labored for days until she finally consented to the surgery to have me removed.

As they prepped my mother for surgery and handed her over the consents to sign, she let out a resounding squeal that caused everyone in the delivery room to focus on her.

"He's coming!" she screamed.

Apparently, I was ready to make my debut after being so stubborn for the last three days.

"Push! Push!" the doctors yelled in anticipation of my arrival.

And just like that, after two pushes, I was officially a member of planet earth.

They proceeded to clean me up in preparation to hand me to my mother.

After I was wrapped in a warm newborn blanket and still crying crocodile tears like most babies that are first born due, I was handed over to my proud mother.

"This kid is just full of surprises! Welcome your little baby girl Mrs. Edwards!" the doctor said as he handed me over to my mother.

"Wait! A girl? I thought it was a boy! Are you serious?" my mother cried as she stared at me while I sat restlessly in her arms.

"I am positive. We probably mistook her for a little boy due to the way she was positioned the majority of the time during your pregnancy," the doctor said.

I can only imagine the anxiety my mother had as reality set in that she had a brand-new baby girl. She was not prepared at all regarding having clothing for the new addition. If I had been born a boy, it would have probably been easier for my mother, especially since she and my pops' finances was not the best. She could have put me in my brother's hand-me-downs that she still had boxed up in the attic. Also, she would have been familiar with how to raise boys since she already had two. Sometimes I reflect on me not being a boy was a set up possibly for all the hell I could endure as a little girl, fatherless in this cruel world. Besides, my thoughts initially would have been that boys tend to be more resilient if placed in a situation to cope with an absent father.

On a lighter note, my grandmother was elated to finally have a granddaughter.

I recollect my grandmother telling me stories of how she came to the hospital to see me in the cold of a new year. She mentioned how snow covered the ground, but she was anxious to get there to see another blessing from God.

Once the smoke cleared and the excitement of me proving the doctors wrong subsided, my mother politely reminded the doctor to tie her tubes expeditiously. Her perfect little family was complete. She was deadly serious about never giving my father or any other man, for that matter, any more kids.

My father was back working, doing his parental duties with us, which entailed helping my mother get some rest by tending to us and bringing things upstairs to my mother as she needed them. My father made bottles at three in the morning and woke up with me on those few occasions when my mother didn't respond within seconds of me crying. However, that did not last long. As I got older, around three months, my father resumed staying out at night. The house was more peaceful when he wasn't around because when he did come home, he hallucinated and paced the house all night.

And just like that, he was back to his *old ways*.

My father took a turbulent turn for the worst as his drug habit consumed him. At one point, he was a functional addict, and he could still work a full-time job. Now, he was back to selling enough drugs to only support his habit. The only reason he worked "real" jobs throughout the years was because my mother fussed about him being in the streets hustling too much.

Some nights, my father would come in the house so high off crack-cocaine, he'd slide couches in front of the doors. I was too young to remember his actions, but my older brothers were not. They would be startled out of their sleep by his demonic actions, and they would run and hide out of fear while he beat on the walls in the house and cried out to his dead father.

He screamed that his dead father was in the room. He struck my mother for the last time one evening amid one of his rants. When he was high on street drugs, he envisioned her being his dead daddy and flashed back to watching his father beat his mother. He was mentally unstable and took his phantasms out on my mother. He cried and banged on the walls of the house, sometimes leaving fist prints in the drywall. At times, this behavior took hours to dissipate, where he would fall asleep in the middle of the living room floor. Other times, my mother, fearing for our safety, called authorities, and he would be detained.

My mother was at her breaking point, and could no longer tolerate him putting his hands on her.

By this time, my uncle was old enough to educate my mother regarding how bad off my father was with his rage and drug addictions. My uncle knew my father was addicted to crack cocaine because they had been indulging in this dependency together. My uncle was ten years younger than my mother, and my father was his only father figure. Therefore, my uncle became a product of his environment and eventually started to pick up all my father's bad habits. They started lacing marijuana to smoke, and anyone that has ever gotten high before will keep chasing that initial *high*. The habit graduated from marijuana to sniffing powder to smoking crack-cocaine. My mother was oblivious to that street life, and thanks to my uncle educating her on my father's drug habits, she now knew the severity of my father's habits.

But little did my father know that he could no longer physically abuse my mother by beating on her. She paced the house while he was passed out on the bed, face up. Her mind raged at the thought of him not only endangering her physically and verbally but subjecting us to becoming motherless if things got out of hand during a violent dispute. He could have hit my mother in the head in the wrong area, or she could have fallen and hit her head and died, leaving us without a stable parent. Little did my father know, this would be his last time putting his hands on my mother across the board.

She waited until my father was fast asleep, then placed cotton in between his toes and set them afire.

He woke up overwrought, and that redbone with a hair full of rollers looked him dead in his eyes, holding an ancient revolver pointed dead at his temple.

"If you ever put your hands on me again, you will go meet your *Maker!*" she warned.

After that night, my pops managed to stay away as much as he could. He only ever came into the house to change clothes in the daytime when he knew we would be elsewhere.

The less he was around, the more peaceful it was.

After my third birthday, my father's drug addiction was so bad that he resorted to pawning items in the house to support his habit. As a family of five, we shared an automobile that was predominantly in my father's possession while he toured the city, fulfilling his desires, smoking crack-cocaine, and several other things we could only imagine. At this point, we had lost our only mode of transportation to repossession by the financing company, and we were still on public housing. Even though this was not the ideal situation, my mother had to utilize government assistance so that she could afford a roof over our heads. At the same time, my father experienced the tragedy of an anesthetized mind.

My mother had a standing warning to my father: If he went back to prison, we would not be around when he returned home.

"Ha-ha-ha-ha-ha. You will never go anywhere, Terri! Besides, *who* would take you with all of these kids?" he mocked.

The final straw was when my father pawned my car seat. My mother was livid and fed up. She asked my father to leave, and he squared up and got ready for the fight. Yet, he knew she was low-key crazy and would do anything to protect her children, so he left peacefully.

As he approached the door with a half-full trash bag of belongings, he turned to her and said, "If you are done with me, I am done with those kids."

My mother was content. She was the epitome of a go-getter, and she had already endured so much, she was not worried about being on her own with us at all.

We remained on food stamps, and we also continued to utilize everything the system offered to survive.

Months had passed by without a word from my father, and my mother was perfectly okay with that. She was finally in transition to get her life on the right track by first going back to community college and completing her GED.

My mother then enrolled at the local Community College and pursued being a Pharmacy Technician. Many local women in the hood attended this Community College to qualify to work in a trade after dropping out of high school once they regained their equilibrium after being a teen mom. A four-year degree at a traditional college was not feasible for my mother, so she thought since she was already living in the hood with three children, she would conform to her environment. The state was giving away scholarships for single mothers to get certifications and/or continuing education in hopes of eventually severing the need for public assistance. She was determined to get us out of the hood and make it happen by herself, and with the help of God, she knew nothing was impossible.

My uncle's addiction consumed him as well. He was the only caregiver she trusted with her kids. Crack-cocaine was the new epidemic that hit the streets, and it engulfed the community. Therefore, my mother didn't have reliable childcare, so she would pack us up, put me on her back, and make my brothers hold hands as we walked four miles of sidewalks together so she could attend classes. My brothers were well-behaved, and they sat in the back of the classroom. You never knew they were even there! The professor was a single mother as well, and thus, perfectly fine with us being there while my mother attended to her studies.

My mother graduated top of her class with honors and landed her first job at a major hospital as a Pharmacy Technician. Pharmacy technicians work with pharmacists to help prepare and give out prescription medication either in a clinic, hospital, or drug store setting. They also take prescriptions over the phone and in person, work with health professionals and customers, help mix medicines, count pills, measure medication, and label and give instructions for medicine, and take payments as needed. Things were getting better for us gradually as my mother started working and got a couple of paychecks under her belt. They started her out at twenty-nine thousand, and that was a major jump from being on public assistance. Now, my mother could afford to go to the mall and buy us Nikes and decent clothes versus shopping for us at the Goodwill.

One day my grandmother offered to keep us one night while my mother went out to enjoy herself. My grandmother was not your typical grandmother because she was still young and spent a lot of time in the streets herself. She loved gambling and playing poker, but occasionally she would sacrifice her nights out to entertain us. My grandmother had the jerry curl hanging down her back with a pecan tan complexion. She was heavy-set and very top-heavy. My brothers used to make jokes about how they would walk in on her trying to put her bra on, and that would totally gross them out.

"Get out of here, you bad ass kids!" she yelled, frustrated that she volunteered to keep us.

I was never the issue, but she thought my brothers, especially the middle boy, was terrible with his behavior.

Because I was so young during these times, I vaguely remember what our activities entailed while we spent the evening with our grandmother. Typically, she would fry us fish and allow us to stay up late watching all the new movies of our choice until we all passed out on the floor in front of the television.

My mother had the urge to go out on the town, hit some juke joints, and have fun with friends that she made on her job. She was invited out by a colleague to this venue called the Ship-A-Hoy in Hillsborough, and she danced all night. Some of her favorites were dancing to Cherelle's hit, "Saturday Love" and Michael Jackson's "Billie Jean." The Ship-A-Hoy was truly a hole in the wall where they fried fish, pork chops, and chicken in the back of the club. The entry was only five bucks to get in, and you could dance all night up until six in the morning. That was one of the safest venues in the city, and my mother's colleague undoubtedly expressed that to my mother before inviting her out. My mother did not get out much, so she was concerned about safety and things that your typical clubber would not be concerned with. She was a mother first, and she looked forward to getting back home to our little faces in a shielded state.

My mother had a brick house shape, and she stayed with one of those colorful, spandex cat suits. She turned heads in the club, and every man there wanted her, but could not have her. She noticed this young, brown-skinned brother checking her out after Queen's "Another One Bites the Dust" song went off, and he followed her to the bar.

"Excuse me, Miss! My name is Keaton. May I buy you a drink?" he said.

My mother was not much of a drinker but would sip on gin and tonic this night.

"Sure," she smiled.

My mother played hard-to-get by flipping her hair and looking past him, acting as though she wasn't interested. Eventually, she accepted the gin and tonic and even graced him with a dance after she had slurped it down. I can see my mother now dressed in an all-white cat suit with lace baby doll socks stuffed into a black pump. Knowing my mother, the heel on that pump was not too high so that she could maintain her conservative look. She was rhythm-challenged, so her dancing entailed standing in one spot, winding her body, and snapping her fingers to the beat. Or possibly, doing "the bump" to a faster song while smiling and showing all thirty-two pearly whites. They were inseparable the entire night, and it was love at first sight in Hillsborough, North Carolina, in the late 1980s.

They dated for six months and experienced a few challenges while trying to outlive the negativity their relationship generated in others. Like the rest of us, they had their tough seasons, but they survived to see their own spring. Keaton's family had a lot to say about him dating my mother because she already had three kids from a previous relationship and felt as though he deserved "better."

"There they go, acting like they're going to make it," the family would mumble under their breath when my mother came around to family functions.

My brothers overheard my mother repeating those hurtful comments on the phone to her colleagues one evening. When my brothers shared that with me, I felt offended. What did they mean my step dad deserved better? *Hell, my mother was better*! She had three children that she took great care of, she was a mother first before anything else, she knew what it looked like to make sacrifices, she was genuine, she was loyal, and most importantly, she was pure.

"Oh, she must be delusional if she thinks he's going to stick around with all those kids," Keaton's drunk sister would say while rocking back and forth in a recliner.

When my mother went on dates with my step dad, she'd drop us off at the green house where my grandmother threw back shots. It helped her get used to this "new thing" because my mother had not dated anyone since my pops left.

"Where are you going, Terri? Out with that pizza man again?" she would laugh while she was almost at her climax of being a lush.

I am just thankful that my parents survived the "lie" that said it was impossible to be loved because of your past or if you have kids outside of your current relationship. They ignored the dubiousness, had faith in each other, and truly did not care what others thought. They knew what they had. They had built a foundation so solid that any seeds of discord someone attempted to plant withered instantly.

Six months into dating this gentleman, Keaton proposed to my mother, and she happily accepted. She mentioned my step dad to us a few times and expressed to us how good he treated her, and she knew that we would like him. My brothers and I were pretty receptive to anyone that was going to treat our mother like the queen she was, so we were excited to see her so happy. Before Keaton, we grew up watching our mother cry over not being able to pay bills, over the electricity cutting off, and the many layers of heartache that my father inflicted. We did not officially get to meet my step dad until a week before he proposed to her. My parents decided that they should wait until their relationship was solidified before bringing Keaton around us. Knowing my mother, under no circumstance was she going to have a rotation of men around us unless it was someone that was going to be a vital part of our lives.

At that time, my mother was still legally married to my biological father, but we had not heard from or received any type of communication from him in years. I was six years old when my mother finally stopped setting up my brothers for disappointment every time they dressed up and waited for our father on the front porch. At some point, as a parent, you must step in and protect your kids. After that last day of waiting, my mother promised my brothers that she would no longer allow him to hurt us.

In time, we just moved on. We had birthdays. We had Christmas. Cold days and sunny days came and went. We moved on and left my father in the shadow of those dark days.

I was in first grade at this point and my mother was engaged to this new man. But where was my father? While I thought about this new male role model and the failure of my father's presence, my mother wondered how she could marry without an official divorce decree. She needed to find him to obtain a divorce, but he was nowhere to be found.

My mother scouted the local jails in Durham, North Carolina, for a month. Eventually, she was informed by a relative that he was in the state of South Carolina, serving a five-year jail sentence for his role in some robberies. I was so young that I don't recollect him being in and out of prison at the time. Once my mother confirmed that my father was indeed incarcerated in South Carolina, she filed for divorce and had the paperwork sent to the prison. My mother thought that this would be the perfect time to obtain a divorce because my father did not have any grounds to fight back. He had not been present in our lives within the last year or so, he was addicted to drugs, and he had an extensive record of being in and out of prison. My pops made the mistake of not taking my mother's threats of leaving him if he went back to prison seriously. He thought that if my mother could only see him, she would have a change of heart and reconsider divorcing him. He knew my mother was loyal, faithful, and would ride for him as she previously did. My mother's character was not to kick anyone while they were down, so she was attempting to scare him straight from ever returning to prison again. Therefore, he contested the divorce, and my mother was petitioned to travel to South Carolina to have her divorce granted. She and Keaton traveled to the hearing, where my father greeted them in an orange suit, a tired face, and handcuffs.

The judge allowed my father to plead his case. He told the judge how my mother was keeping the children away from him, so he had not seen us in years. My mother represented herself and made her case to the judge that her husband was estranged, that she had not heard from him in years, and assumed that he simply did not exist. He had never reached out to her anyway, nor did he check in on us. All she wanted was stability, and for a woman and her children, a chaotic marriage gives less peace of mind than just a clear-cut divorce.

My father scanned the audience and realized my mother had brought a fair-skinned fellow with her to the courthouse, and that is when it hit him that she was serious.

"Is this seriously what you want to do? You actually want to divorce me?" he whispered.

My mother flipped her hair and looked over her shoulder at my father with a smirk on her face.

"Judge give her whatever she needs so she can move on with her life! Bailiff let us go!" he said out of anger.

The judge granted the divorce, and everyone parted ways. That meant a fresh start for all of us. My mother had met an amazing man who would now raise us as his own and give us a better life. We would have an active father in the home, and that was something that I needed as a little girl. My brothers, who were four and eight years older than me, had witnessed so much chaos between my biological parents, they were numb and reluctant to embrace all aspects of stability. As the youngest child, I never got to build that rapport with my biological father. Therefore, my step father was all that I knew as a father figure.

A few months later, my mother had my father served with termination of rights paperwork for him to sign. Termination of Parental Rights means that a person's rights as a parent are dissolved. The person is not legally the child's parent anymore. The parent also loses the right to visit or talk with the child. In addition, the parent has no say in any of the aspects of how the child is raised. That leaves an opportunity for the child to be adopted without the parent's permission.

Courts typically take away parental rights to protect children that are in unbelievably bad situations with their custodial parent. It is rare that a parent can start a process to take away the parental rights of another parent. However, in this case, my mother feared for our safety because he had become so violent and belligerent. Upon his release from prison, my father could have attempted to kidnap us, and my mother would have had no legal ground to stand on to prevent it. I was never clear on the reasoning behind her decision, and I never asked as I grew older, but have always trusted my mother's judgment. Also, I do not think my father had the mental capacity to be in our lives. So, he signed the paperwork, and we never heard from him again. The fact that they never had the opportunity to co-parent successfully was going to be challenging for us kids. Because this was not an option, I feel as though my brothers and I were going to potentially be raised with some sort of void and/or possibly harbor anger towards our biological father. Fathers solidify identity and foundation in their offspring. The unfortunate part is we would likely never know "who we really were" without that missing piece.

We could assume that our father just loved getting in trouble with the law by continuously committing crimes more than he loved us. However, I think the initial plan was for my step dad to adopt us since he was going to be the one caring for us mentally and financially moving forward. He was going to be taking on an additional three kids that he would have to learn and get to know daily. He knew that there would not be any additional monetary support flowing through the household since my father had signed over his parental rights. My step dad voiced to my mother on several occasions that he signed up to take us in as his own when he married a woman with three children. He was adamant that he was taking on everything that came along with a *ready-made family*. Nevertheless, the adoption process was not vital during our transition into being a blended family, so they just opted for him to raise us as his own, and it worked out.

My mother and step dad were married a month later at the justice of the peace, and they were happily in love. Love for them included feeling for the other that goes beyond any selfishness or self-interest on the part of the loved one. As such, love nurtures and has a positive effect on each person's self-esteem and sense of well-being. Love never involves deception because misleading another person fractures his or her sense of reality. That is something that my mother longed for while she was married to my biological father. My step dad treated her with the utmost respect. He displayed such tenderness and showed so much compassion in all areas of her life. I remember going on camping trips to the cabin during the summer, and I would doze off on the floor watching all the latest comedy shows: *The Jefferson's*, *Three's Company*, and

Happy Days. I would literally laugh myself to sleep and then wake up to wander around the antique cabin that stood three floors high in the middle of the woods. I will never forget there was this incredible open patio area on the second floor that connected to the living room, and that is where I would find my mother and step dad. She would be facing the woods overlooking the pond, and my step dad would be holding her so tight around her waist. Sometimes I would just stand there and gaze at how much he loved her. My mother had endured so much with my biological father, and I was just thankful to God that He gave her back all the years she lost fighting for something that she should have let go of a long time ago.

Life took a three-hundred-and-sixty-degree turn for us. My step dad was an accountant major at North Carolina Central University back in 1983, before meeting my mother. My step dad was two years younger than my mother, but he had experienced a lot more than her academically, being independent, and being exposed to the nightlife scene. Working full time had afforded him the opportunity to not resemble your typical college student by hosting parties at his apartment and partying on a nightly basis. Although he was determined to finish his education and follow in his other three sibling's footsteps, he opted to give up his studies to pursue a management career in a pizza franchise business. So, before he even met my mother, Keaton was stable and embracing the bachelor's life. I did not think it was a great decision for him not to finish his education, but he was happy managing the pizza franchise, and he was particularly good at it. Keaton was very structured, organized, and a people-person, so he thrived and successfully moved up the ladder within a year of being in the business. He was making about $35,000 a year back in 1983, which would be around $90,000 in 2020. Taking care of his new family was not an issue. Besides, my mother also worked, and two incomes will always be better than one in a bustling household of five.

Keaton also had children from previous relationships with two different women. His son was my age from a previous long-term relationship, and he had a baby girl on the way when he met my mother. Details about the new child and her mother were never discussed in front of us; that was kept private between my parents. I remember overhearing conversations about finances associated with the amounts that would need to be paid for both children and, at times, it got heated.

From what I gathered, the co-parenting relationships were not the best. My step dad's son did not come around us initially. Once Keaton was married to my mother, he received child support paperwork for his son. Keaton informed the mother of his daughter that he did not want to have a romantic relationship with her. However, just like his son's mother, Keaton knew child support paperwork would be in route to him as well. My step dad didn't have any hesitation when it came to monetary obligations, and he was eager to be an active and engaged dad. Active dads are individuals that are not only providers, but they put just as much time into a kid as the other parent does. They attend games, ballets, partake in first words, watch their child take their first steps, and are also involved in the decision-making process. Active dads do not leave the mother alone to raise a child on their own.

After my step dad went to court for his daughter, he was ordered to pay $500 a month in child support. Her mother and Keaton's relationship wasn't the best, and my parents said that his daughter wouldn't be allowed to visit with us until further notice. That was not good news for me growing up in a house full of boys. Even though I enjoyed the athletics and roughhousing with my brothers, a part of me longed for a softer side. I thought maybe a sister would be perfect for filling this void. But from the looks of it, it was not happening any time soon.

Later, his daughter's mother relocated to Greensboro and began a new life there, raising her daughter.

When it comes to child support, I feel that if you are paying for a child, you should be allowed some type of visitation rights. Even though family court is a separate entity from child support court, if you can show documentation for payments for your child, you should also have the same access to them. A lot of men do not have a desire to be in court, let alone attempt to fight someone for joint custody. Therefore, in the end, it does a child a disservice not to have both parents being active in their lives.

Chapter 4: Step Fathered

My step dad moved us from Durham, North Carolina to a town called Butner, which was about forty-five minutes away. Coming from the city of Durham, Butner was the country for us city kids. There were tons of open land, lots of trees, and red mud. This town was excessively slower than Durham, and every landmark (like the supermarket) was fifteen or more minutes away from us. As we drove through the town to get to our brand-new home, I felt sad. I was going to miss all my friends, and I had to meet new ones. Even though we all had to start over, I was being selfish and was only concerned about myself and how I would adapt.

Reflecting on my mother's decision to move us to the country, she made one of the wisest decisions thus far. Durham was starting to become a high-crime and drug-trafficking area, and my mother refused to raise us in that type of environment. She began to see young boys, my brothers, Saul and Barak's age, dropping out of school, and standing on the corner selling drugs to their elders. It was all about sacrifices with my mother,

73

and even though this permanent move would be better for us, her commute to her job increased by forty-plus minutes.

As we drove past an immense amount of greenery on the way to our new living space, I heard the groans come from my brother's side of the car.

"Where are we?" my oldest brother groaned as he stared out the window in disgust.

My mother ignored his negativity and proceeded to drive to our new destination.

Even though the city seemed severely boring in all aspects, it was a major upgrade for us to no longer be on public housing. My parents had purchased a brand new single-wide trailer, and everything in it was brand-new. When you first walked into the trailer, you entered the living room. I stopped and looked at the wallpaper of little pink roses that covered the walls in its entirety. The carpet was dark brown and so fresh I took my shoes off so I could feel my feet sink into it.

"We've never had new carpet before!" I exclaimed as I smirked at my brothers.

I knew they were just as irritated about the move as I was, but I was trying to make the best of it. Besides, I was a kid, and I did not have the option to live and pay bills on my own.

When you went to the right, my bedroom was the first one on the left. It was very tiny, but I was glad to have my own room, so I did not complain. My mother enticed me on the drive here about how my room was so spacious, and I even had my own walk-in closet. Before this house, I shared a room and a bunk bed with Barak, so this was a major upgrade for me. Walking a little bit more down the hallway, I discovered the bathroom my brothers and I would share and their room on the far right. I ran back through the living room to meet my mother in the kitchen.

I could tell she was happy, so I'd tell her later that my room could have been a little bit bigger.

"Go check out my room, Tabitha!" she said as she cried tears of joy.

I walked back through the living room and caught my mother with her hands propped up on the countertops and her head hanging in between her arms. She rocked back and forth, silently praising God for this new house. That is what she did when she was overwhelmed with joy and thankfulness.

"Aww, mom, I'm so glad you're happy," I said as I grabbed her and hugged her tight.

I turned out of the kitchen and made a left into her bedroom, and it was a sight to see. Coming from the projects of South Durham, we resembled *The Jefferson's* regarding the "moving on up" soundtrack. I fell in love with her garden tub and silently made plans in my head to fill it up full of bubbles and bath salts the first chance I got.

I always wanted a daybed because it was not bulky like bunk beds, and I liked the way it would not clutter your room, so that is what my mother got me. Besides, that was the only thing that was girly about my entire life. I looked on the bright side as I continued walking through our brand-new home, my brothers still had to share their room. I guess there were some perks to being the only girl.

I noticed a tremendous change in my mother's life, as well. My step dad's family was heavily involved in a local church close by, and they were advocates for having a relationship with God, so that also affected us. I had not grasped the whole idea of this God thing and felt like it was being forced on my brothers and me. The realism that a greater presence existed was foreign to me, especially since "church folk" seemed so mean and uppity. Aunt Mildred was always ushering and passing out the envelopes for people to submit their tithes and offering. She was one of those uppity people that I am referencing. I always felt as though she looked down on my parents because they both had kids from previous relationships out of wedlock. I'd catch her staring at me from across the room at family functions, and it made me uncomfortable. Aunt Mildred was educated and very business savvy. She and her husband had opened their own accounting business after they graduated from college, and anything opposite of success was not even an option for them.

My step dad's mother was on the hospitality board, so she was always involved with banquets and receptions at the church. These were more functions that I was forced to attend. For some reason, it seemed as if I was the only young lady in a dress that despised these events. I isolated myself and played in my plate of food all night during these gatherings until it was time to go home. My step dad's mother's name was Lior, and that is what my brothers and I called her. We refused to call her grandmother because we did not want our biological grandmother to hear that. She did not play that and was adamant that we only had *one* grandmother, and it was her.

The food was decent, considering my step dad's mom stalked my mother for all her recipes. I remember waking up to the smell of collard greens and a honey bun cake baking on a Saturday morning and knew my step dad's mother was in the kitchen with my mother acquiring some of those raw cooking skills.

My mother started making us go to church with them, and we could not refute it because we were underage at the time. I was a few months shy of eight, my middle brother was twelve, and my oldest brother was knocking on sixteen's front door. Then, my brothers got to the age where they refused to go, but she made me go because I was the only girl, and I was younger than my brothers. My mother did not seem to think that dressing me up and parading me to the church while Saul and Barak were lounging at home was a double standard. I mean, she made me wear dresses and all. One dress that I hated was purple and white striped with pleats in the skirt. I was tortured in real-time by being forced to dress like Mary Poppins, and if that wasn't bad enough, a colossal number of pigtails sprouted out from all over my head. If you were to walk in my parents' house right now, that is the 20 x 30 picture you would see displayed above the fireplace. So, on this particular Sunday, not only was I her guinea pig, but we even had a mini photoshoot with my step dad, my mother, and myself. My brother's better be thankful they dodged that bullet.

The ridiculous attire and hairstyles she made me wear were not the only things that embarrassed me. I did not understand why my mother would jump up after the preacher said something, start to speak funny, and lose control of her bodily movement at times. I mean, my mom was not the only one that behaved like this; my step dad's family did it too.

Aunt Mildred was supposed to be ushering, and the next thing you know, she has been held up by another usher because the spirit had jumped on her. But no one topped my mother's two steps and her fallouts. My dad would attempt to hold her up, so she would not hit the floor while the spirit jumped on her. I can see his face now, trying to remain calm and acting as if my mother's behavior was totally normal as she wrinkled up one of his Steve Harvey suits, before Marjorie.

I did not see the need to attend church every Sunday and Wednesday night for bible study. Plus, I did not have a relationship with my mother's God, so maybe that's why I didn't understand any of it or care to for that matter. Then we had our traditions for after church where one person, typically my mother, was designated to cook at our house. She rushed back home to the pots she left stinking so good the morning of and disappeared in her room. I knew this meant she was going to wash up and get into comfortable clothing to finish preparing Sunday dinner.

She returned to the kitchen with a made-up face from church and her clip-on earrings. One of my mother's light Sunday dinners entailed fried turkey, fried chicken, meatloaf, collard greens mixed with mustard greens, candied yams, sweet potato pies, honey bun cakes, neck bone, rice and gravy, potato salad, cornbread and a smorgasbord of food spread all around the teal marble countertops. Soon, my step dad found his way in the kitchen to help her prepare for his family to arrive. They still had to finish up paperwork from tithes and offerings, and possibly their usher board duties before the family showed up. So, my mother had two hours to burn before church folks and laughter filled the house. I watched my step dad and the way he catered to my mother. Despite my young age, I was in awe of how much someone could love a person. I wondered if this would one day be my love story, and then I would quickly snap out of my daydreaming at the thought of a boy even touching me.

Chapter 5: Spaulding

My step dad is the only dad I knew, so he is and always will be "dad" to me. Sometimes God places people in your life that you have absolutely considered family; that has nothing to do with your lineage. Although Keaton lacked the emotional attachment that my brothers and I needed, he was a provider, and he gave us anything we wanted. I grew up with boys, so I was a tomboy at heart.

We all played basketball, and we were tremendously talented.

I played the position of power forward, and I was a beast inside the paint. I wasn't much of a shooter; I was more of a defender than anything: rebounding, blocking shots, catching bricks and putting them back in the hole, a shitload of assists, and intimidating the other team to pass instead of shooting the ball.

Being a defender in sports related to my real life. I had to defend myself from my older brothers, who gave me a tough time by making me fight neighborhood kids and always telling my mother that I was doing things that I wasn't supposed to be. Plus, I felt as though I had to be a defender about my biological father not being around. I assumed one day I would grow up and display certain behaviors of having *daddy wounds* from him being absent from my life, and I would have to defend myself as well.

The knee-baby put a basketball in my hand when I was just shy of five years old, and I've been nice with it ever since.

I went on through elementary school and then to middle school with a love for the sport. My favorite basketball player of all time was Michael Jordan. I thought he was the best basketball player in the entire world. He also played for the University of North Carolina in college, and he was a Tarheel. He was significant to me because I was a North Carolina native. Michael Jordan's story also resonated with me regarding how coaches denied him and did not see his potential prior to him arriving at the University of North Carolina. They counted him out, and he overcame all the negativity and made a name for himself in the history of basketball. Therefore, I planned to make history in some form one day, just like Michael Jordan did.

We played in the summer leagues at the Sports Arena and stayed involved in anything associated with basketball. I remember jogging almost a mile every day (the majority of the time alone), dribbling my basketball to get to practice. All I was into was Spaulding, so that's what the neighborhood called me.

Spaulding was my first love and the first real thing that I could call my own. I was gifted to play basketball, and no one could take that away from me. Spaulding was patient and kind, and contingent upon how hard I trained, Spaulding would show up and reward me during game time. I became obsessed with all aspects of the game, and that is what I buried myself in.

I was a little different from the other girls that were in my age range because they were into boys and having sex. I don't remember much sex education in school. Our curriculum was pretty much cut and dry when it came to general education, so maybe they were getting educated in their homes by their parents. Most of the kids that I interacted with had both parents in their household. In our small town, promiscuity and outlandish sexual behavior were popular. The mothers were so oblivious to these types of sexual behaviors, and by the time they figured it out, the girls were too invested to quit and/or they were already pregnant.

At the time, I did not have a desire to date or entertain anyone of the opposite sex romantically. Besides, I felt as if I was way too young, and no one was interested in me anyway. My self-esteem was at an all-time low because I did not think I was pretty, and my hair was not straight. The pretty girls in school wore Dominican blowouts, and their hair had lots of bounce to it. My hair, on the other hand, was always pulled back in a ponytail because I played sports. You don't have to be confident to have sex, all it takes is two willing parties, and it's done. But I was not willing, not yet at least.

Therefore, I buried myself in educational and urban books, along with sports. Low self-esteem can be associated with young girls starting to have sex. For example, you have a young lady, such as me that does not get any attention. Then, one or two boys start to show interest, and they manipulate you into thinking you must give up the goods to keep them around. I had too much pride and dignity to get caught up in that hype, so I kept my teammates close and distanced myself from most of my classmates.

Somehow, I realized it was okay to be different, to stand for something, and know that I had more to offer than just my panties to these little boys. If all the girls were giving it up that easily, what made me any different from them? The goals of the other girls were to hook up with the hottest guys in school and for them to be an item and/or the hottest couple in school.

For some reason, the girls at school did not care for me; I wasn't quite sure why they hated me so much. I tried to make friends with them, but they would just turn up their noses at me.

I sensed early on that I would be the female in her late twenties with no childhood friends. According to society, if you do not have any childhood friends as an adult, you cannot be trusted. I didn't know how true that was since one of my peers repeated a conversation that she overheard by ear hustling her parent's conversation. The hell with that myth, especially since I was the outcast in this small town. You guys do not even have a population of two hundred citizens and dare to be territorial.

Some of the young lady's boyfriends started to flirt with me, but I was not interested. I dressed just like the boys, and I was not cute at all. For the most part, I was super slim, flat-chested, and resembled a little boy, even in the way I walked.

They were only interested in me because they could smell fresh meat. The girls tried to fight me on several occasions. I would arrive home from school to three or four girls standing in my yard. It got so bad that my mother had to step in because it seemed like every single day I was outnumbered. One day, my mother pulled up early from work and saw five girls in the yard, who asked her if I could come out and talk to them.

"You sure can talk to her after I change my shoes, so I can help her beat the brakes off, you guys. If all of you want to fight her, either you can go get your mama's, so I can fight them, or I will handle all of you!" she shouted.

There was complete silence as I stepped out on the porch in my practice clothes to see why my mother was yelling my name from outside. Once they realized that my mother was a little banana crème pie ready to unravel at the first glimpse of a threat, the yard emptied instantaneously. Like hyenas, they scampered away while they muttered their vow to get me eventually. My mother could not protect me 24/7; they knew that, and I knew that.

One day, a month later, my mother had to stay late at work, and she could not pick me up from school. That made me an easy target on the bus. I was so frightened that I phoned my mother at work, and told her their plans to jump me. But the superhero I expected to rescue me from the hyenas took a raincheck. In fact, my mother scolded me for calling her at work with petty girl drama. But I knew she wanted me to be my own hero, to stand up for myself, and to handle my business. If I did not, I would get my ass beat by not only the girls, but by my mother as soon as she got home. She worked too hard, after all, to raise a rug of a daughter.

I only had two hours of school left that day, and it seemed like the longest two hours of my life. One of the girls was my classmate, and she just kept punching her fist in her palm. I envisioned her fist punching me in my face when the bus reached our stop. Every time I turned around, her violent presence imprinted on my frantic mind. Surely the bus driver was not going to allow this to happen. She giggled and talked about how I was going to get what I deserved, even though I had not done anything wrong for these girls to hate me.

The bus driver turned out to be more of an instigator than a protector. In her early twenties with acned pale skin and a razor-like, brunette Mohawk, she wore fitted baseball caps, so we never saw her eyes as she looked up from the road into the rearview mirror.
Even the bus driver was in cahoots with that gang of girls; she was the older sister to one.

As we loaded the bus that day, I tried to sit close to the front where only one student occupied the seat, but the students in the front refused to let me sit by them. They were all in on the beat down that was allegedly about to take place when we got off the bus. The gang of girls strategically spread themselves out on the bus. Sitting at the front of the bus would have made an easy escape. All eyes were on me as I walked towards my doom at the back of the bus.

The ringleader of the group was a girl named Portia. Portia stayed in trouble at school and made a name for herself. If you messed with her, you'd reap the repercussions of getting beat down by her and her crew from the rough trailer park. Portia stood five-feet-two, had very dark skin and was not easy on the eyes. She did not look very intimidating to me, but she was stocky and built like a little man. And because I was so scared and had never been in a fight without my brothers present, I was not looking forward to our stop.

I began to hate my mother's job because they switched her to the evening shift, which meant she couldn't pick me up from school per our routine. However, when I spoke to my mother earlier on the phone, I sensed she was fed up with these girls harassing me, and she wanted it to come to an end, even if that meant I had to defend myself by finally fighting back.

Whatever mechanism inside of me that held the threats, name-calling, and dirty looks, suddenly released, and created a pulsating rage. I began to smell blood. All I could think about was what my mother told me over the phone. I feared my mother more than I feared these chicks, so I had to act quickly. I waited as everyone exited the bus, and I got off slowly behind them. I stopped at the bottom step to see six girls waiting to fight. Mind you; I dressed like a boy, always in a hoodie, basketball shorts, and some sort of fly Nike sneakers. Thank God I wore the Timberland's that day. Timb's were very thick and could be used as a weapon to stomp someone. If I were able to get one of the girls on the ground, I could use my Timb's to stomp one of them out, to show the other girls that they didn't want *this* problem. Instinct took over, and my body began to move without thought. I dropped my book bag, pulled off one of my Timberland's, and began wielding it around and flailing my arms, like a bat-shit crazy baton twirler. I ignored my tears as I accepted that looking crazy and unpredictable was my best line of defense. I was all alpha animal, as I scanned the crowd, daring anyone to meet my glower, and attempt to rush me.

Nobody moved. They looked on, silently. My madness empowered me as I shouted, "Whose first?!"

No one moved. Were these girls afraid of being knocked upside the head with some heavy Timb's? All this fuss, the bullying, the threats, and now none of them would step up? I continued to look at the growing crowd. I *wanted* someone to challenge me, to make sense of this craziness that consumed me. Were they really scared? Or were they just watching me lose my mind?

The girls avoided eye contact and looked away. So, I spun around to understand, had I become this intimidating? It felt good, but my transformation was unbecoming—would I have to live up to this part forever? Would I go from Spaulding to Timb's?

I looked up, and I saw the real master of this deranged role. This was his stage, not mine. I could have been lying down on the concrete, and none of these girls would have touched me. But here I was with one shoe off and a wet face. My middle brother,

Barak, stood behind a house, watching and waiting for me to get jumped. He could pick on me, be mean to me, and treat me like crap, but nobody else had permission to do the same. And if anyone ever challenged him, all that could be done was to pray for mercy.

My brother was always my protector. Like Moses parting the sea, Barak walked from behind the house and motioned for me to start walking towards him. An immense amount of peace came over me as I retired the role of the deranged girl and came back to being Tabitha.

"I watched you the whole time," he said.

We were off the stage. I was back to being Tabitha, but my mother was always the director. She was behind the scenes making sure we got through these acts of life. She spoke to my brother to ensure he got off the bus before I did, to make sure I wasn't scared of them, and to make sure I got home safely.

He wrapped his arm around me as we walked towards our house.

"I was waiting to see if anyone was going to try to harm you. I was going to jump them. I don't care Tabitha; I was going to fight all of those girls for you." he said. "Now, put your shoe back on."

Chapter 6: Her

After that day, life was peaceful as I rode the bus for the remainder of the school year. My mother was proud of me. Those girls never bothered me again, and any debris of fear temporarily left my body. That was the beginning of a gift and a curse.

After that incident, I spent more time alone and disposed of thoughts that I should attempt to make friends in my new territory. Not only was I loner because I didn't have any friends, but watching the other little girls interact with their dads as they got picked up from school stirred something in me.

Samantha was an exceptionally beautiful little girl with her hair in pigtails down to her butt. And she always dressed like a princess. Samantha wore tutus, shiny shoes, and glittery shirts depicting lots of hearts. Classmates on the playground said that she was in ballet and aspired to be a ballerina one day.

Her dad went the extra mile when he picked her up from school. He'd jump out of the car and run to pick her up. Before he placed her back down, he would spin her around while showing all thirty-two of his teeth.

After they had their father/daughter moment, he opened her car door to make sure her seatbelt was strapped tightly before returning to the driver's side.

Where was my biological father? Like, what part of the world was he in? Also, why didn't he want to pick me up from school?

"Mom, where did my name come from?" I asked.

I always wondered why my mother did not name me something simple, like Christina or Samantha. I wanted to know where this seemingly peculiar name came from, especially the spelling.

"Actually, your father named you," she said quietly.

That unnerved me.

"You mean the father who doesn't exist? Who is he, mom? Where is he? Why didn't he want to be in our lives?"

At this point, I thought that maybe he lived this lavish life and my brothers, and I did not fit into his lifestyle. Perhaps he was remarried with kids, and his new wife didn't want us to be around.

My mind began racing, seeking answers while I waited for my mother to respond to my questions.

"Tabitha, your father had an issue that handicapped him," she replied after a significantly long pause.

Handicapped? I thought to myself, "I didn't know he was handicapped. Was he in a wheelchair? Did he walk on crutches? What type of physical handicap did he have?"

She continued, "He wasn't mentally stable enough to be a father at the time. That is part of the reason why we're no longer together," she said.

Stable enough? So, he had a mental impairment, huh? Interesting. Why would she have married and carried kids by a man that wasn't mentally stable?

None of this made sense to me, and I was very mature and intelligent for my age.

In addition, if that was *part* of the reason why he didn't stick around, what were the other "parts?"

My mother was careful and tactful with her responses when I started asking these questions.

Besides, she never wanted to bash my pops.

But that did not help me. I got angry because my mother tip-toed around the answers that I needed.

"He's a piece of crap for not wanting to meet his kids!" I would yell out periodically.

Looking back, I think my mother felt as though I was too young to know all the moving parts associated with why my father wasn't around, so she gave me just enough to soothe whatever rejection I was feeling at the time.

But she never knew, it did not help me at all.

I didn't know who I was. I lacked identity. Identity is typically associated with fathers. And because I felt fatherless, I had internal issues that surfaced at an early age.

My mother said things like, "Your father loves you and your brothers very much, Tabitha."

She spoke to always protect the slight chance that I may eventually meet this stranger, who probably looked like me, maybe moved like me, and could have had the same eyes as me. It is an odd thing knowing that someone out there in the world had the same blood as me and didn't care to know what my voice sounded like, what my favorite color was, or what I dream about at night. I dwelled on whether blood meant anything. Here I was with my mother, feeling partially whole. But during moments like this, I felt fractured. And my mother knew that. She treated the mention of my father as if she was speaking about me. That is how forward-thinking my mother was. Yet, she never deprived me of the truth, especially my truth.

My brothers did not give a damn about *that man*, but I was genuinely curious about my roots.

Where was his family, and why didn't they reach out to us? My mother was not the type to ever keep them away; it just was not in her character. So, what was their issue?

Once I knew my name was attached to my pops, I wanted to change it. He was the worst person on earth for leaving us alone in the world without considering how we would protect ourselves or that he was replaceable by a step father.

His absence began to dig at me. All he left me was a name, a word, a sound people make that I reacted to. I did not want to answer something given to me by a person I did not know. Every day, I completed my assignments in school without writing my legal name on my papers. I was in the early stages of an identity crisis, and the teacher started asking for conferences with my mother.

At the conferences, my mother insisted that I was perfectly fine. She did not see any harm in me wanting to change my name; she understood my strife and confusion. But just as she insisted that nothing was wrong with me, she equally insisted that his name would always remain my name. I told her I would stop, but I never could embrace a name from someone who had abandoned me.

Ms. King was one of my favorite teachers and the only teacher who cared about me outside of the classroom. She was my homeroom and English teacher, and she is one of the reasons I fell in love with writing, pronunciation, and learning those formidable words that I had a desire to learn. Ms. King always made sure I participated in the yearly spelling bees, and she gave me all the tools I needed to prepare for the competition. In addition, she told me how beautiful my name was and even tried to dissect the meaning of it.

She also gave me tough love when she realized I was turning in my papers with different names on them. I had severe identity issues, and I did not like myself after questioning my mother several times about my father. I felt like a piece of me was missing, and I didn't know who I was because I didn't know who my father was.

After class one day, Ms. King told me if I did not stop, she was going to start giving me zeros since the name on my paper did not exist on her class roster. Because I cared about my grades, and I was so competitive with a girl in my class named Tessa, I stopped. Tessa was brilliant as well, and she always wanted to run over to my desk after we got our tests back to see what I got. The majority of the time, her grades were only one or two points higher than mine, but I was not content with that. I needed to study harder and surpass Tessa on all levels, so I started reading the dictionary.

When I first asked my mother for a dictionary, she was in total shock. But because she was determined to fuel my dreams and aspirations to be the best, she went and purchased the most expensive Webster she could find. So, when I was not playing ball, I was balled up on my daybed, highlighter in hand, reading the dictionary word-by-word and then writing the word in a sentence.

The morning after my dictionary-reading sessions, my mother always asked, "What's the word for the day, genius?

And I would happily respond. "Charismata!" I shouted. "Because she stood out, her charismata aided her into opportunities that weren't necessarily available to others!"

I was always skittish when speaking to my mother, as I straightened my shoulders and dropped my hands down in anatomical position because I wanted to impress her.

Even though she didn't always verbalize how proud she was of me, I could still read her body language.

I was the most focused and dedicated child she had, and she was continually pouring into me daily, whether it was on our rides to school or when she was making dinner.

Chapter 7: Can We Talk?

My life changed as I walked down the street one day to basketball practice. I saw this hot, popular guy from school, maybe a couple of years older than me that I normally passed in the halls on a daily basis. There was no reason to think that *he* would notice *me*.

He called me by my first name.

"Tabitha! Hey girl, where are you going?" he asked.

"How do you know my name?" I asked as I stopped in the middle of the street still bouncing my basketball.

"Trust me, I've had my eye on you for a while," he smirked.

I was so nervous because he was the most handsome guy at school. His name was Korey G., and I must say, he had the most amazing white teeth I'd ever seen on a man. His skin was dark and flawless; clearly, he was fresh off the runway with the gear he had on.

"I'm headed to basketball practice," I replied.

"Can I walk with you?" he asked.

Now, this was not your average teenager asking little old me out. He was only the most popular, best-looking guy in school, and he wanted to walk with *me*!

"Sure, if you want to," I shrugged.

He ran down the hill and walked the mile with me that was ahead.

All of a sudden, I wasn't able to string two words together, so I started rambling. It was love at first sight.

Korey G. walked me the entire way to basketball practice as I bounced Spaulding. He asked me about my interests outside of basketball and how I got started in the sport.

"I can tell you have the passion for the sport by the way you talk about it," he said.

He told me bits and pieces about himself but only enough to keep me wondering. He was very inquisitive and seemed interested and interesting.

When we arrived at practice, I handed Korey G. my ball as he walked to the bleachers.

I could feel my coach staring as I threw my practice jersey over my white V-neck t-shirt, and jogged to the basketball court to begin stretching with my teammates.

Six-foot-three Coach Eddie was of black and Indian descent. I guessed he was in his late forties because he had two kids that were a few years older than me. He was always dressed in black or grey windbreaker pants paired with a Tarheel's hoodie. His thinning black hair was styled in an unfortunate comb over. A stern look was always planted on Coach Eddie's face during basketball practice. He would get upset if you didn't listen to a play avidly and begin to breathe heavy out of frustration in regard to us not listening to him. His response to our shortcomings would startle the entire team which naturally forced us to engage more. Because our basketball team was compiled with a plethora of natural talent, sometimes we felt entitled to do less while we were in practice.

Coach Eddie continued to stare at me while we started shooting around, and I knew exactly what was going through his head. This new boy following me to practice was going to be a serious distraction. I'd played summer league for years, and my coach had never seen a boy with me, let alone accompany me and stay to watch practice. I instantly understood his frustrations because I was his star player, and he wanted to keep me focused. But I didn't care because I'd just met him, and he was not affecting my basketball skills... so I thought.

"Get back, get back!" Coach Eddie screamed as I lost focus when Korey G. exited the gym.

My mind raced. Where was Korey G. going? Maybe he did not like me after all. Just that quickly, a young man can throw you off track. I lost focus for a split-second until I heard Coach Eddie calling my name.

"Tabitha! Get your head in the game!" Coach Eddie yelled.

It seemed like Coach Eddie was always yelling at me about something, so I snapped into focus and started listening to plays that the point guard, Martie, called out.

My mother was not going to be pleased that Korey G. was seventeen, and I was thirteen. But I didn't care. I genuinely believed this was love. And I was falling.

My heart raced as he returned to the gym with two plastic bags and sat back down. Coach and my teammates looked to see who was at the gym door. By then, practice was over, and I couldn't wait to walk back home with him. Korey G. walked up to me and pulled bottled water out of one of the bags and offered it to me. I was mesmerized. It was the sweetest thing ever.

As the weeks passed, we spent more and more time together, and I ended up falling for him hard. My brothers grew wary of me hanging around this older guy and told my mother that some young man had an interest in me.

Clearly, they were unhappy and did not want me to be happy. My brothers didn't have girlfriends, so they just wanted to make my life miserable. Or maybe they wanted to be overprotective brothers, but this was not the time for that, especially since this was the first guy that genuinely had an interest in me.

"Who is this boy you've been running around town with?" my mother asked, her face twisted with disgust. I always knew when my mother was serious because her stance was very still. Then, she'd prop one hand up on her hip, and her voice deepened.

"You've missed your streetlight curfew three nights in a row, and I am sick of it! Since you cannot seem to follow directions as your brothers do, you are grounded!" my mother growled.

"I hate you!" I yelled as I slammed my bedroom door.

I had no idea why my mother was so mad at me. Wasn't it natural for me to like guys? Especially since my grandmother had planted a seed in my mother's brain that I would end up being a lesbian since I did not like *girly* things. I guess every female that played basketball would be a lesbian, according to my grandmother.

All I knew was, I was not a ballerina, and I surely wasn't about to wear any tutus to school.

This is who I was, and they were going to have to accept me as I am.

The next morning, I found out the real reason why I was grounded.

My brothers had told my mother that Korey G. was the city's player and all he wanted to do was get in my pants. Also, they said that they heard in school that he had slept with more than ten girls, and that is what he was known for.

My mother's anxiety began to arise within her because this seemed familiar to her. *Was Korey G. going to be my "maroon Camaro" like my biological father had been to her at one point in her life?*

My mother had to put an end to that, so she grounded me from the phone. I had my own phone line, but that was removed from my bedroom as well. All I could do was go to school, basketball practice, and go back home.

I was physically sick. I could not talk to Korey G., and the entire world was conspiring against me. What was Korey G. thinking? I was nervous and anxious because so many girls were after him. I saw the way they looked at him in admiration and then looked at me with disdain. It would be easy for him to move on. Maybe he would start thinking I was too young for him, or that he could do better. All types of toxic thoughts consumed me as the days without Korey G. turned into weeks. For some reason, he had not even attended school. Even after two months of not speaking to him, I was still in turmoil. Just the thought of him set off a whole array of emotions.

I dreaded the end of practice because I'd become sad. Usually, Korey G. would be there to walk with me home, or we'd eat dinner at my favorite Chinese restaurant.

"Hey, pretty lady," a familiar voice said as I exited the gym.

It was Korey G. defying everyone who was trying to keep him away from me. He snuck up there to see me. I ran and jumped up on Korey G. He was wearing a blue Adidas hoodie, but I could spot him anywhere. Wow! I was shocked Korey G. had come to see me! So, he *had* been thinking about me the entire time.

"Oh my God! How did you get here? My mother is going to kill me if she sees you," I exclaimed as I looked around nervously.

He motioned towards a green sports car parked in the open lot outside of the sports arena. One of the things that Korey G. and I had in common was a passion for muscle and sports cars.

We walked to the car, and he opened the door and motioned for me to get in.

"Whose car is this?" I asked.

I noticed it was a 1993 Ford Probe hatchback coupe sitting on a beautiful set of low-profile tires. It was money-green with grey alloy sports wheels, and it looked as if the springs had been burned because it was lower to the ground than the average Ford Probes.

"Mine!" he said.

"Wow! This is so dope!" I yelled with excitement, then wondered how he could afford it.

"I'm not coming back to school. I got a job at the mental health facility as a patient care technician in Butner right after we stopped talking," he exclaimed.

Butner, North Carolina, was famous for their mental health facilities, warehouses, and prisons, and drew many of its residents from other areas of the country. You had a *good job* if you worked at one of these places.

"I'm going to work, save my money up and take you away from that evil family of yours," he said excitedly.

Korey G. felt that my family was evil because they were using every means humanly possible to keep me away from him.

That was music to my ears, given how strict my mother was.

Minutes later, a green Mazda MPV pulled up. My mother was here, and I had to leave.

"What are you doing with that boy? I thought I told you to stay away from him! He is way too old for you!" my mother hollered, as I climbed into her van. I was foaming at the mouth with rage.

"Mom, you haven't even given him a chance! He is nice to me. Look at me! Boys do not like me!" I screamed. I always had my hair pulled back, I always wore baggy clothes, and I never felt cute! Anyone paying me attention was beyond me, and I was not about to lose his attention.

"He likes me, mom! He calls me beautiful. He wants to buy me nice things. Please give him a chance. Just say you will meet him…" I begged as we pulled away from the center of my teenage heartache.

My mother drove quietly as Korey G. got smaller and smaller in the rearview mirror. Silence has never been my friend, so I held my breath and watched, hoping she would share her thoughts. Despite the rumors my brothers heard about him, Korey G. treated me nice. *So what if he had a past?* Everyone does at some point. Should I hold him accountable for a history with other women, even though none of its debris was ever evident while we're together?

She finally said, "You know what? You're right. I haven't met him. Instead, I've been making decisions based on what your brothers told me. If I try to stop you from seeing him, you are just going to sneak anyway, and I do not want a relationship fueled by deception for you. So, let's invite him over for dinner and see how it goes."

I was the happiest girl ever! I called him as soon as I got home and shared the good news. Korey G. was excited, but appropriately nervous because he was afraid of my brothers. Saul and Barak were both at least six-foot-two, and they didn't play when it came to their little sister. While Saul was more on the slim side, Barak was solid, and his weight shifted at times. Their complexions were both a notch darker than mine, and they were quite easy on the eyes. Saul was reserved and largely stayed to himself. He was most verbal when he was gaming with Barak. That is why I was so surprised when he had so much to say about me dating Korey G. and took this information to my mother. That was Barak's role, to snitch on me for whatever reason.

The reason Saul was so worried is that most of the girls at our school had reputations for being promiscuous. I'd overhear my brothers talking in their room. One time they referenced a girl named Rasheeda who had a gorgeous pecan-tan complexion and an oversized booty. She walked through the halls and threw her body on every athlete she passed. Rasheeda's strategy was to switch her hips and purposely drop her books as male athletes headed her way.

Because there were few females at the school to choose from, most of the guys didn't care how many boys hooked up with Rasheeda. The more the boys dragged her name through the mud in the locker room, it made other boys curious to know what she was working with.

My brothers were not like those boys. A lot of girls pursued Barak and Saul even before we moved from Durham to Butner, but they maintained their integrity and stayed true to their relationship-driven nature.

"It seems like every cute girl I'm interested in has already hooked up with two or three guys that I know," Saul said.

I wished they knew there was no reason to worry about me being like these other girls at school. Sex was the furthest thing from my mind, but I did have a massive crush on Korey G. Before I existed in his world, when I saw Korey G. in passing, I got butterflies. He always wore the best gear and the freshest shoes. It left me wondering why guys of his caliber didn't like me.

When someone makes you happy, it's easy to overlook what happened before you became a couple. For example, he was not getting a fair shot at dating me with my family because of his past encounters with the girls in our city. His reputation was known for being the epitome of *hittin' it and quittin' it.* I intended to get to know Korey G. better while hoping that my family adapted to him, even if they didn't accept him as a potential mate for me.

Korey G. was the first guy that wanted to visit our family home officially as my date. I struggled with anxiety and wished I could have had my step dad's input, but he was never home. His sixteen-hour days managing the pizza parlor meant he sometimes missed vital moments in my life. My step dad's absence was just another void, among others that I adapted to.

Not only was Korey G. perfect, but he was punctual, and I knew that would impress my mother. She was her usual happy self while whipping up delights in the kitchen and humming gospel music.

"You just never know what someone lacks at home. So, I always make sure to love on everyone," my mother often said.

First, the doorbell rang, immediately followed by two knocks.

Then, a few lighter knocks followed.

My dinner guest was here.

Fortunately for him, I was not dressed up. I was being myself, and that is what made me feel my best. I had nothing to hide, and I felt even better when Korey G. mentioned that he adored that about me most. I was not trying to be someone else like all these other girls who tried to be grown women.

I wore my mind as I wore my age in my standard attire: basketball shorts, fitted ankle socks, a cut-off tank to show my baby abs that poked through with a sports bra underneath.

I rushed to the door and, just before reaching it, broke my stride into a paced and cool swagger. I took a deep breath to calm down, but my arms chose otherwise. I swung open the door so fast that I almost lost my balance. The doors on our home were flimsy, so rushing to swing it open was never a good combination.

"Hi, Korey! Please, come in," I said.

"Hey gorgeous," he said and embraced me in a hug.

He stepped in and took in our humble home before he noticed my mother standing in the kitchen next to the refrigerator.

"Good evening, Mrs. Edwards," Korey G. said.

My mother never met a stranger and was never formal with people she invited into her home. She always wanted to give people that home-feeling, even when it came down to my friends and teammates when they stopped by.

"Hello, son. How are you feeling today?" my mother asked.

He walked in and greeted everyone pleasantly before taking a seat on my mother's black leather U-shaped couch.

"I'm feeling pretty good today and just thankful to finally meet you," he said.

My mother looked over her shoulder from the kitchen and responded, "Thank you for coming, Korey. I know these types of first-time meet-and-greets are never comfortable, but just know that you are welcomed."

My mother prepared my favorite meal in the whole world: cubed steak, rice and gravy, and green beans. She knew this was my favorite meal, and I wanted to share with Korey G. the things I loved. Normally for guests or the church folk, she'd always freestyle her meals that always entailed three types of meat, four sides, dinner roll or cornbread, and for sure, dessert.

After a while, my mother washed and dried her hands and walked over to Korey to get a hug. As she hugged him tight, she blushed and looked up at me.

As we sat at the dinner table, I came to find out he had a lot in common with my brothers. My mother adored him. She laughed hysterically at all of Korey G.'s jokes. I could not help but wonder if he reminded her of my biological father when they first met. After dinner, we went to my room and played Sonic the Hedgehog on Sega. It was the weekend, so my mother allowed him to stay an extra hour.

Things were finally coming together, and it is all because she decided to trust me. I was not a bad kid at all; I just had tons of issues with self-esteem and insecurity. But Korey G. helped with my rejection issues caused by my biological father. I felt so abandoned, and because my mother always seemed to downplay why my father was not around, I started to resent her. With Korey G. in the picture, I had somebody to listen to me. He was so patient, and he loved me so much that it literally blew my mind. I did not know what I did to be so deserving of his love because the only thing noteworthy about me in middle school was my athletic abilities. But Korey G. affirmed and reassured me that not only was I good in athletics, but I was brilliant and beautiful as well.

I even talked him into returning to school. Education was imperative to me, and I did not want a dumb boyfriend on my team. He told me on several occasions that school was not for everybody.

Apparently, he had been held back in eighth grade twice. Korey just wanted to quit, work full-time, eventually start a family, and be a provider. That all sounded good because it reminded me of my step father. But I wanted more for my life than just graduating high school and working a nine-to-five. At least, that is what I felt in that moment.

I always had a rebuttal and told him that he was not applying himself, and I was there to help him.

He loved me so much that he re-enrolled back into school.

Initially, his family didn't care for me because I was so young, and Korey G. protected me by not bringing me around them. That is what he told me, and I believed him. Korey said his family situation was toxic, and he preferred to be with my family. Besides, he was desperate to prove my brothers wrong and to show my mother that I had his entire heart.

Now that he was suddenly enrolling back in school, his family wanted to know who this "new girl" from Durham was.

One day, Korey G. and I were walking through the hall together in-between classes when a boy in passing said, "Good game number thirty-two!" I processed that as somebody just addressed me as a number. I looked back to see who the boy was and realized it was Fred Jr. from my morning homeroom class.

Korey G. instantly knew what I was feeling, and he intervened. It was almost as if he could feel what I felt.

"Even though it seems as if no one really acknowledges you by name, just know that you are important, and you make a significant impact on people daily!" he said.

I smiled and handed him a letter as we departed to go to our classes.

That was a beautiful beginning of affirmations and love as he read my letter and then reciprocated by writing me one and making sure I got it at lunchtime.

"Korey G. told me to make sure I hand-delivered this to you," a girl said as she walked up to me.

She was shorter than me with a short haircut, big boobs, and booty, very hippy, and she looked like a little doll-baby. Her hair texture resembled mine with the tight curly coils undulated on the side of her hairline into her sideburns, and it instantly made me wonder who she was to Korey.

"Thanks!" I said sarcastically.

My insecurities were getting the best of me since I felt as though this alleged eighth-grader in the same grade as him, was way prettier than me.

I got to my next class, which was science, and plopped down in my seat.

Even though I hated science, it was fun for the most part because we didn't do anything. Plus, there was gossip surfacing through school that the science teacher, Ms. Foster, and my teammate, Diane, had a secret lesbian relationship. I had not been exposed to lesbian relationships, and what it looked like outside of my grandmother saying I was going to be one, so I ignored it.

During class, everyone was doing their own thing while Ms. Foster and Diane stayed in the corner near Ms. Foster's desk the entire time. At times they did look closer than they should be, but that's none of my business.

I unfolded my letter with hearts on the outside and began to read:

Dear Tabitha,

I just wanted you to know that I am falling in love with you, and you

bring me so much joy when I am around you. I look forward to

spending the rest of my life with you, and I hope that we can be

together one day without limits.

Love,

Korey G.

I started to blush, but then had a change of heart. Was this moving too fast? How did he know he wanted to spend the rest of his life with me in such a short amount of time? I was still noticeably young, and I had my whole life ahead of me. But it just felt so right.

The bell rang for recess, and I headed to the playground to play kickball with the rest of the kids. I enjoyed kickball, and it was a great way to keep me in shape for basketball outside of my evening practices. I had a new coach since I'd moved from playing arena basketball to middle school. Coach Jackson was another tough one. I always had tough coaches, and they always gave me a hard time.

As my relationship with Korey G. grew, and I put pressure on him to meet his family.

He finally agreed to take me to his home and introduce me to everyone. I was super-excited because we would be solidifying our relationship.

I spoke to my mother about it the next day, and she was on board with meeting his mother, especially since he spent so much time at our house.

What I knew about his family was his mother and father were divorced, so they stayed in separate households. Korey's brother lived with him and his mother, and he had several dysfunctional siblings scattered all over the city. The brother that lived at home was the oldest out of six of them, and he was struggling with an off-and-on drug habit. That all sounded familiar.

My mother and I arrived at Korey's house around noon on a Saturday afternoon. My mother agreed that if everything went smoothly and the atmosphere was copacetic, I could stay there for a few hours, and she would pick me up later.

"His mother must be home, Tabitha, or you're not allowed over," she said as we sat in front of Korey G.'s house.

"Mom! Don't start!"

"Tabitha, I don't know these people, and you're my only daughter!" she said.

"Isn't this the whole point of us coming here, so we can get to know them?" I asked, rolling my eyes and looking out the window.

The side door of the house opened, and Korey G. appeared in the doorway.

I was so happy to see his face, especially since my mother had already started tripping over nothing. She had not even given them a chance, and I was getting a whole speech. My mother's overprotectiveness at times didn't make sense to me. She never had any issues trusting me, so until I gave her a reason not to trust me, she should give me a little freedom.

"Come in! Come in!" Korey G. said as he motioned to us.

As he reached for my door, my heart skipped a few beats. He was such a gentleman, and my mother was getting to witness it. I was glad he was completely being himself, so maybe she would get her panties out of a bunch!

I cut my eyes in her direction before stepping out of the car as we prepared to enter the house. Even though my mother was very reserved, she was receptive to getting to know the family because she supported me in everything I did. She was my biggest fan!

As we entered the home, we were greeted by a tall woman, about five-eleven, with a long blonde weave. She was glammed up for sure. I had never seen anything like it before in my life.

"How are you two? I am Ms. Jay!" she said as she reached her hand out for a formal shake.

"My name is Tabitha. And this is my mom, Terri," I whispered.

"I know you aren't shy with your pretty self," she laughed.

She moved to shake my mother's hand.

"Please! Please! Have a seat!" she demanded.

Korey G. motioned for us to follow him off into a secluded room.

Tan couches covered in the thickest plastic I'd ever seen filled the room. Giant plants that looked as though they were growing out of the ceiling resembled a jungle. My mother had a green thumb as well, but this lady had her beat!

I sat closely beside Korey G. on the couch as I watched his mother enter the room in a silk night robe, two champagne glasses, and a bottle of wine.

She was truly a diva, and it was not up for debate. She popped the corkscrew on the bottle of wine and began to pour my mother a glass.

"Oh no! I do not dr---," my mother tried explaining to her,

"Oh! Of course, you do! One glass of wine never hurt anybody! Besides, they drank wine in the bible," she added as she looked up at my mother.

Now I was embarrassed and wondering what exactly Korey G. had told his mother about my family.

I watched my mother stare at the glass of wine for seconds before reaching for it and indulging in some gossip about work.

Ms. Jay worked at John Umstead as a patient care technician and had been there for over two decades.

"Come. Let me show you my room." Korey G. said as he reached for my hand.

Every time he grabbed my hand, I would damn-near melt in that moment. He was so beautiful to look at, and most times, he left me speechless. We headed down a dark hall that reeked of incense and lavender. His room's walls were magical. They were covered with posters of the latest artists consisting of Immature and 3LW that had been ripped out of Word Up or Right on Magazines.

"Wow!" I said.

"You like it?" he asked.

"I love it!" I responded.

As I roamed the room, it seemed as if Roger from Immature stared at me behind that patch over his left eye.

His bed was nice and plush as I plopped down on it.

It sat extremely low to the ground, and it did not have a frame.

Korey G. walked over to the door and pushed it closed.

Then he locked it.

It did not make a sound as if he had sprayed some type of lubricant on it to reduce the sound of squeaking. He seemed like a pro.

"How many girls have you had over here?" I asked.

"A few," he responded as he plopped down next to me and breathed heavily down my neck.

"What are you doing? Our parents are in the next room," I said.

"Tabitha, you really have to relax," he said.

I felt like Akeem did on *Coming to America* as he slumped down in the swing.

I was so uncomfortable being alone with a boy for the first time.

"Look, if you're going to be my girl, there are some things you cannot be scared to do," he said.

"I'm not scared of anything!" Little did he know, I was scared to death. Was this appropriate for us to be alone like this? I felt Korey G.'s puppy breath on my neck as his hand slid down into my sweatpants. I tried to jerk away from him, but he held me tighter.

"That feels good, doesn't it?" he said as he rubbed his fingers *down there.*

It felt good in a weird way, but I was not telling him that.

"What are you doing?" I implored him.

"I am making you into a woman," he said.

I then felt pressure *down there,* and I jumped up to my feet so fast, Korey G. almost fell off the bed.

"Just let me put the head in," he said.

I had no idea *what* he wanted to put his greasy head in, but I was not interested.

"I think we better go back in there with our parents now," I said.

I opened the door swiftly and headed down the dark hall alone until I turned the corner into the living room, where I heard an immense amount of laughter, and I saw my mother's peaceful face.

She looked a little pale and flushed, but I did not ask any questions. I was only concerned about getting the hell up out of that house.

"You ready, mom?" I asked repeatedly.

Surprisingly, Korey G. never followed me out of his room.

I wasn't concerned; I just wanted to go home.

My mother sensed my uneasiness because she searched for the keys that were right in front of her. I grabbed the keys and backed up to the living room entrance. I was hoping my mother would get the vibe and follow me out.

"Is everything okay, dear?" Ms. Jay asked.

I nodded and rushed out of the patio door. I unlocked the money-green van and anxiously anticipated my mother coming out the door. Ten minutes passed before I heard laughter getting closer to the van.

I looked up and sighed.

My mother approached the van with her face flushed and looking pale from the consumption of alcohol.

I cut my eyes at the steps where Ms. Jay stood and gave her a quick wave.

"What's wrong with you?" my mother asked.

"Nothing, mom, as long as you had a good time!"

"That Korey G. is a fine young man," she mumbled as she backed out of the long

narrow driveway.

I stared out the window as I attempted to process what had just transpired.
Was he attempting to have sex with me? I was not ready for any of that foolishness. I felt violated in a way and unworthy of *the wait*.

My mother was silent. She was not a drinker, so she was trying her best to keep the van within the yellow lines on the black paved roads as we drove through the city to get back home. We only had a ten-minute ride. Before we could even get into our driveway, I cracked my door open and jumped out of the van way before it stopped.

"Tabitha!" my mother screamed.

I didn't even stop to answer. As I hit the corner of our single-wide home, I made a bee-line to the front porch. I bounded up the three steps and swung open the screen door. Whoever came in the house last had left the main door open. We did that from time to time since we deduced when we first moved there that we were in a very safe neighborhood.

I rushed into my room and slammed the door behind me. I was furious, but I didn't know why. Was sex all he wanted from me? Maybe my brothers were right when they told me that he was known for preying on all the hottest girls and sleeping with them. Maybe I was furious because I did not want them to be right.

I fell back on my daybed with my shoes still on my feet, and I stared at the ceiling for hours.

I was used to Korey G. calling me throughout the evening after school. But tonight, there were no calls. Wait! I knew why! My brothers and I shared a phone line, and my parents shared the other phone line in the house. Maybe my brothers were on the phone talking to one of his high school crushes. I picked up the landline phone, and the dial tone reverberated through my head. Korey G. didn't even call to check to make sure my mother and I got home safely. I was devastated, but I was *not* going to reach out to him. Besides, that was not our routine for us to not communicate via phone once we parted ways. I would always let him know that I was in the house safely, vice versa.

I was kind of sleepy as well, but then I began to wonder why my mother didn't check on me. Sometimes I just needed her to come in, sit on the edge of my bed and tell me everything was going to be okay, even if I refused to tell her all the intricate details about what happened. I did not have that comfort level of telling her *everything*, and I thought that would come with time. But it was embarrassing to share certain things with her without being ridiculed or frowned upon. Even though that was my mother's parenting style, and she was a great mom, it was not what I needed just then.

I must have dozed off while my brain was doing backflips because when I woke up, it was time for school. I was starting to dread going there because basketball was stressful, I had to compete with other girls for Korey G.'s attention, his constant defense of me from the mean things other girls said about me, and the substantial school load itself. As the bell rang, I hurried to my homeroom, with only seven minutes left to get there. I was just in time and took my seat close to the back. I dropped my book bag down next to me and looked down at the scribbled-up desk. These desks were ancient and disgusting.

Typically, we sat in homeroom for twenty minutes and then switched over to our first class, which was Math for me. I anticipated the bell ringing, so I could creep over to the eighth-grade hall to see if I could spot Korey G. As soon as the bell rang, I darted out of the classroom. I fought through crowds and cliques of students chit-chatting until I saw the top of Korey G.'s head. He was standing at this locker, and as I approached, I realized he was not alone.

"What's she doing with you at your locker?" I asked him as I stared at the girl he huddled over. The girl was the same one that I used to see him with in the halls—the one with the big old booty.

"See. She has what it takes to be my lady," he smiled as he looked down at her.

She was substantially shorter than him, barely reaching his hips.

"What's that supposed to mean?" I asked as I felt tears cranking up in my eyes.

"I don't need a little girl. I need a woman. And this is a woman," he said and stroked the side of her chin.

I fought an unprecedented uncontrollable rage and managed to stay calm.

"Korey G., like what's going on? Can we talk after school? Can I please come to your house?" I begged him.

"School. No! This is my last day of this foolishness. I only came back to attend school because of you. It has never been my thing. I have a job, a car, and I'll have my own place soon. School isn't for me," he said.

I stared at him in complete despair, racking my brain for where I went wrong.

Granted, this girl was prettier than me, and she was known for getting around with all the guys in school. And then it hit me like a ton of bricks! It was all about sex. No sex meant no phone call and no respect.

Unfortunately, I was not there yet with wanting to make out, so if he was going to hold that against me, maybe I was not the one for him.

The bell rang. That bell meant that I was late for my first class of the day.

At that point, a crowd began to gather, and I was not the one for making a scene, so I left.

I held my head down the entire time as I made my way back to the sixth-grade hall. Then the tears started to flow uncontrollably. "This was not and could not be the end," I thought to myself. I cannot let this loose tramp take *my* boyfriend, and I would have to redeem myself. I had to conjure up a plan, and it had to be quick.

I was broken for the entire day. It's nearly impossible to function and be productive when your heart has just been shattered into a million pieces.

I went to basketball practice that evening, and I could barely focus.

"Tabitha!" Coach Elliot screamed.

I sluggishly made eye contact with him.

"Get on the line! Pay attention! Catch the ball!" he yelled.

I was tapped out mentally, but this was my dream, so I needed to focus. I dreamed of playing professional basketball, and this behavior of being nonchalant and not hustling was not going to get me there.

I got on the line and proceeded to run suicides. "Get on the line" was never a command you wanted to hear as a basketball player from Coach Elliot. You had to do sets of suicides in the middle of practice while everyone watched. And if you kept messing up, the entire team would have to do suicides as a whole, and your teammates would be furious with you.

Coach Elliot was a new addition to the team and a tad bit younger. He was not with the shenanigans of horsing around on the court. He had played college basketball somewhere in the Midwest, and he was dedicated.

Something in me shifted after I ran two sets of suicides, and I was back and focused.

"Why are you so hard on me, Coach Elliot? I'm just a kid!" I chuckled.

"Come with me," he motioned towards the locker-room.

I walked in behind him as he shut the door. I sat on the floor in his office and slipped off my sweaty Nikes.

"You want to know why I am so hard on you?" he asked.

I just stared at him as I sat Indian-style and rubbed my feet. They were extremely sore, and I was trying to relieve them of the pressure after running suicides on top of my routine practice drills.

"I'm hard on you because you're one of the best. I see the potential, but I just need you to stay focused. You told me this was your dream, right?"

"Yes, sir!" I replied as I sat up straight.

"That's why I'm hard on you. You don't need to focus on that boy. Do not lose sight of your aspirations, dreams, and goals. You're playing at this level in middle school, just imagine what your potential will be in high school. At the rate you're going, you'll get a full scholarship to college because of your talent."

I wasn't sure how he knew about Korey G., and I wasn't going to inquire. I just avidly listened to him as he criticized my poor choices. I felt compelled to rebel and tell him to stay out of my personal life, but I did not.

"And you are probably wondering how I know about that boy. Listen, it's my business to know about all of my players and what they have going on in their personal lives," he said.

I thought to myself, *Was this guy psychic like my mom? How did he know what I was thinking?*

"Your mom is out there to pick you up, so head on out and remember what I told you. I'm going to stay on you!" he said to me as I exited his office.

I jogged to the bleachers and grabbed my gym bag with my shoes in my hands. My mother was standing at the door, waiting for me. She usually waited in the van outside, but because I was not out there, she must have come inside to look for me.

"Hi, mom!" I said.

"Hi, Tabby. Where were you? You know I've been at work all day, the least you could do is be ready and waiting for me outside, so I won't have to come in," she said.

"Coach was talking to me about my potential and how I need to stay focused," I said.

"He thinks you're that good, huh?" she asked.

"Yes," I responded.

My mind drifted for a second to playing college basketball, being on my own in unfamiliar territory, and having to start all over. It gave me anxiety. Being that far away from my family would be a challenge. I quickly snapped out of it when I realized I had years before I needed to even address some of those fears.

"You are that good, Tabby! I want you to know that. You can and will do anything you put your mind to," my mother said.

"Thanks, mom. That really means a lot coming from you," I replied.

I adored my mother. She was going to always have my back and ride for me. I could not thank her enough.

I walked into the house slowly, feeling weak from practice. I walked straight to the bathroom to shower and then attempted to call Korey G. for some answers about the stunt he pulled today in the halls.

After my shower, I headed into my room and closed the door. I was not even hungry. All the drama from school today decimated my appetite, which was a rarity since my mother's cooking was unmatched. She could cook almost anything, and it was seasoned not only with perfection, but with love. Therefore, if I was missing one of my mother's meals, it had to be serious.

I laid across my daybed and reached onto the floor to grab my red landline phone to call Korey G.

It seemed as if the phone rang for an eternity before someone picked up. All I heard was breathing on the other end.

"Hello?" I said.

"Yeah," Korey G. said flatly.

"That's an interesting way to greet your girlfriend that you've ghosted for a few days.

"Girlfriend? Tabitha, I told you what was up with us at school. I need someone who can give me what I need not only emotionally, but physically as well. You are *not* that girl. I know that now, and it's okay." His tone was reassuring.

"No! I can fix this!" I cried out.

"Face it! You're a little girl, and we're not in the same league," he said with more bass in his voice.

"But wait..."

The line went dead.

I tossed the phone across the room and sobbed.

How could this be happening? For the first time in my life, I felt loved. Someone finally liked me, and I had to go and ruin it.

I didn't know the first thing about sex or how to make it happen. I was distraught. I was angry. I was livid. But I had to fix this.

My mother was eating at the dinner table when I said, "Mom? Do you mind driving me to Korey G.'s house? My notebook is in his book bag, and I can't do my assignment without it."

"What do you mean you can't do your assignment?" she asked.

"Mom, please. Can you just drop me over there so I can get my notebook? You don't want me to fail English, do you?"

My mother was huge on academics because she dropped out of school to run from state-to-state with my biological dad. And she didn't want the same for her kids. But my mother also didn't know how to tell me no.

"Tabitha, it is almost nine o'clock," she said.

"Then don't worry about it then. If you don't care about my grades, neither do I."

I rushed into my room and slammed the door hard in hopes that she would notice.

And she did.

After throwing my other books onto the floor and tossing the landline phone into the wall, my mother opened my bedroom door.

"So, you don't get your way, and you're tearing up my house?" she asked.

"Mom! I really need my notebook! Besides, Korey G. is saying that he isn't coming back to school for a while, so I will not be able to get it from him. My assignment is due this Friday," I pleaded with her.

"What do you mean he isn't going back to school? Is his mother allowing this to happen? I don't know if you should go over there fooling with those folks!" she said.

"Mom! Please! Why do you care what other people have going on in their households? Korey G. told me everyone isn't school material, and I believe him."

"Actually," mom said and leaned against the doorway, "that's pure laziness and a lack of ambition! Everyone needs to have an education to progress in life."

I was neither intrigued nor interested in a speech. I just needed to get over to Korey G.'s before I lost my boyfriend to some sloppy, big-booty chick.

I wanted to give him whatever he needed, and I needed him to like me again.

My mother disappeared from the doorway.

I huffed and puffed and threw myself back onto my daybed. What happened to the Korey G. who was utterly smitten with me? The one that vowed to protect me and take care of me? This couldn't be right. How could a boy who put in all of this time and effort with me just snatch it away? I craved how secure and wanted Korey G. made me feel. That was my drug.

Was this how my bio dad's drug addiction felt?

Chapter 8: High School Woes

I entered into high school, pushing down feelings of intimidation. It was so different from middle school. Even the blue-trimmed glass doors loomed tall and opened to a sizable lobby. Our school mascot was a Viking, and for me, blue was a masculine color that symbolizes strength, wisdom, and stability. On the right, four large wooden doors led to the school auditorium. I passed the principal's office and the cafe where all the seniors hung out during lunch. This felt different, but I'd finally made it.

The girls walking the halls to the auditorium looked foreign with their straight hair, makeup, and strutting in high heels with a twist in their step that was out of this world. Their designer clothes included Parasuco jeans that accentuated all the right curves to get that hourglass shape.

As I passed them to get to my first-period class, they laughed obnoxiously in that snobby way that only mean-spirited girls could achieve. You knew it when you heard it.

"What is she wearing?" a short-haired girl said as everyone busted out laughing.

Then somebody said, "Hey! Leave her alone, that's Saul and Barak's little sister."

My brothers were good-looking and relatively new faces that stayed to themselves. Pretty boys that were quiet drove these girls crazy.

"Oh! What's your name? Are you really Saul and Barak's little sister? Where are they? I haven't seen them in a while."

Little did they know that their paths would never cross because my brothers were no longer attending school. They had become a product of their environment.

Saul wrestled with the spirit of entitlement because, according to him, my mother didn't send us to school in the best clothes. When my brothers turned sixteen, she stopped buying their clothes and shoes because they were old enough to work for the things they wanted. That was my mother's attempt to instill value and responsibility in them at an early age, but it backfired. Saul thought it was my mother's fault that he couldn't afford designer clothes, and if he couldn't wear designer clothes, he didn't want to go to school. Therefore, according to his theory, my mother caused him to drop out of school.

Barak still got up every morning to leave for school as scheduled. However, he listened to Saul's gripes and complaints on the daily about not having the latest fashion and on how whack school was. Besides, sleeping in and playing video games all day was tempting.

As a result, both dropped out of high school.

My mother deemed it a generational curse. It was such a waste because my brothers were super-smart and talented in basketball. University sports agents and recruiters scouted Saul during summer conditioning and while he played throughout the school year. There was not a math problem too hard for Saul. He helped me with my homework on many occasions because math was not my strongest subject. Barak struggled with dyslexia in an era when teachers either didn't know better or didn't care and just passed him on to the next grade. I felt there was room for him to apply himself more.

My brothers opted to work with my step dad at the pizza parlor making $8.75 an hour. Saul delivered pizzas while Barak cooked.

In the meantime, I was determined to see basketball through, and I was not going to waste my talent. My brothers taught me everything I knew about basketball, they passed that torch to me, but I was the last one standing school-wise. Coach Jackson, my middle school basketball coach, had two observations about me: One, I had an immense amount of potential. Two, I had to get rid of my attitude. I was scouted in middle school, so all I needed to do was maintain good grades, practice hard, and stay focused.

Now that I was in high school, something was happening with me that I couldn't put my finger on. Classes were slightly more difficult, but that was attributed to my eighth-grade counselor signing me up for gifted classes. Ms. Nelson thought those classes would look great on my high school transcript, but I never really wanted to be in those classes in the first place.

How were all of these people so sure that I even wanted to go to college? Everyone seemed to be making plans for me, except me. With everything I had endured, I really had no clue what I wanted to do after high school anymore.

All of my middle school friends were adjusting just fine and loving every bit of high school as freshmen. Me, not so much. All of the changes and the increased pace of high school triggered my anxiety. Sitting in classes for extended periods with pressure to excel in this final stretch before college was exasperating. My obsession with Korey G. obliterated much-needed focus so that my days were spent sitting in class, just waiting for the bell to ring.

There was a rumor going around school that Korey G. was dating an older chick who lived six houses down from me. I acted as if I didn't care. But deep down, I was hurting. These older chicks at school would say, "Sis, you're just going to let that cougar take your man like that?" Maybe they were in her age bracket since she wasn't in high school anymore. I had no idea if she graduated or dropped out, but I did know she had a young child from a previous relationship.

Ironically, she worked at a sister pizza parlor to my step dads. She showered Korey G. with brand-new Jordan's, all the new Karl Kani and Fubu attire, and paid for his frequent visits to the barber. All he had to do was ask.

I overheard my step dad telling my mom about a worker that was possibly stealing from the pizza parlor. My step dad stayed in the loop with all the managers at the sister stores, discussing staff, company news, and management strategy.

The thief had to be the cougar. She looked just like trailer park trash with her dry bob, her faded jeans, and her shirts stained with dry baby vomit. Now it made sense how she could afford to keep Korey G. materialistically satisfied. If I told him she was a thief, maybe he'd stop entertaining her.

Even though Korey G. and I had not spoken in a while, I still felt as though I was owed an explanation especially with the way things ended between us. I had to confront him with this newfound information that I had ear hustled from my parents.

"Hello," Korey G. answered.

"Are you dating that ugly girl that stays around the corner from me with all of those kids?" I asked him.

"Who? Me? Hell no! That chick is hanging with my sister, Finnie, and I know she likes me, but I'm not even thinking about her!" he assured me.

"I am hearing rumors in school from complete strangers that you two are dating. Is she giving you sex and that's why you have since ghosted me?" I asked.

"You cannot question me. But if it gives you any peace, the answer is no and I am not seeing anybody Tabitha. And you actually caught me as I was walking out of the house so I will talk to you later," he said before hanging up in my face abruptly.

That wasn't good enough. I needed to know the truth. Unfortunately, truth-finding took away from my studies. The cougar's cousin, Shea, stayed across the street from me.

"Hi Shea," I said to her one Saturday morning, bouncing my basketball in the middle of the street.

"Tabitha! Why are you on the street at nine on a Saturday morning bouncing that basketball?" she asked.

"Did I wake you up with the noise?" I laughed.

"Yes, you did! You do this every Saturday morning." She was annoyed.

But I didn't care about her sleep; I only cared about getting some answers about my boyfriend.

"Well, I'm waiting on my boyfriend, Korey G.," I said to her. I dropped his name to see if Shea would react.

"Your boyfriend?" she scoffed. "Yeah, right. That's my cousin, Tiara's boyfriend."

"Girl, bye! Korey G. told me he doesn't even like her." I stopped bouncing the basketball.

"Hell, you're out here waiting for him, and he's at Tiara's house right now! He has been there since seven this morning," she said.

My heart dropped into my stomach.

They say be careful what you wish for, but at that moment, I wished I were the wise man that never said nothing at all. I rushed back home and slammed my bedroom door. That lying, cheating bastard! I ugly-cried myself into a long, deep nap, awakened by my phone. I managed to ignore the calls until they became back-to-back in the afternoon; I knew it was Korey G. I promptly took the phone off the hook, so he'd get a busy signal.

I stayed in my locked bedroom the entire weekend and felt sick at the thought of him being with that ugly girl and felt equally sick at the idea of not talking to him at all.

Despite feeling completely depleted, I went to school when Monday rolled around. The school receptionist announced over the intercom system information about basketball tryouts that day. I ignored them.

What was I doing?

This was me, the same person who dreamed of attending Grambling State University to play basketball. I guess my mother's God had plans unbeknownst to me. Sometimes we believe that we are making our own decisions, but my mother's God possibly had His hand on my life the entire time. So, I wasn't really giving up anything. It was not in my plan to be a professional basketball player I attempted to convince myself.

It was literally downhill from here. How else would I learn my own momentum?

Chapter 9: Who is that?

I started to realize that Tabitha was becoming someone else. And that didn't sit well with me. I was at the dawn of my conscious life, still learning and growing as I eyed myself in the mirror every morning and wondered who was staring back at me. Her hair was getting wilder. Her shoulders were setting into the frame of a young lady. Her eyes were hungry for more, and whatever she had right there in the mirror was not enough.

The way I was growing with Korey G. felt like a weed rather than a flower. I felt desperate to root myself between his rocky lies, and as a result, my sense of self was spread thin. I was never meant to live a shallow life; there was too much history rooted in me. There was too much upheaval and struggle from prior generations for me to just sit down and settle.

The one in the mirror said *this is it, Tabitha.*

And I was horrified and thought, *I am more.*

I was losing myself in the murky waters of what it meant to be Korey G.'s girlfriend. The honor, respect, and dignity that had always been part of me had somehow crumbled and blew away. I didn't know how to negotiate my being. I felt disoriented and misplaced, and that terrified me. I didn't yet have the words, but I knew I was in a toxic off-and-on relationship.

To my surprise, Korey G. didn't come by, but I saw him in passing as he drove to Tiara's house. Korey G. had placed racing pipes on his Ford Probe, which must have been trending. So, I could hear his car coming up and down the street, whistling and taunting me that I was just another girl in another house on his checklist.

I sat alone in my room, wondering if he lost interest because I wasn't spontaneous enough. Maybe I was boring, or perhaps I was too young. What did these other girls have that I didn't? As I stared at the wall and thought about how to win him back, the most desperate and disparaging ideas raced through my mind.

If I would have given in that night to his demands of sex, I could have told him I was pregnant.

One of my teammates told us about how her sister lied and told this guy she was pregnant after he broke up with her, and he took her back. As fast as the idea emerged, I rejected it. Besides, I didn't know anything about getting pregnant. And wouldn't you have to get fat at some point? And who would want to have kids anyway? All they do is cry and poop everywhere.

One night, I was lying in bed with the usual background noise of mom clanging pots and pans, and my brothers' heavy steps shuffling against the shaggy carpet. I resolved to mentally cut ties with Korey G. and not take his calls ever again. I told my mother to tell him I wasn't home if he decided to ever stop by again. Even if he called her line when he couldn't reach me, she was to inform him that I was not available. I unplugged my phone and tossed it into a drawer. I was going to reciprocate that same energy and ghost him the same way he did me!

Weeks went by without Korey G. I started staying after school to shoot around with my former teammates. They had all made the basketball team, and they were upset that I had given up basketball. Coach Ellis, who followed us to high school, asked me every day to join the team, but my head was no longer in the game.

Basketball was a passion, but I respected the fact that being on the team meant I had to invest one-hundred percent of myself. My one-hundred was gone. I didn't want to mislead my teammates, so I gave it up. I didn't want to disappoint people, the same way I'd been disappointed my whole life. Not knowing half of my roots meant I'd never have a complete picture of my identity, what was expected of me, what was possible in life, and what hopes and fear pulsed in my blood.

Candice, one of my previous teammates, was extremely rough around the edges. I at least had my hair up in a messy bun while hers was wild, dry, and on edge as if a ghost had just spooked her. There were some days Candice would not even brush or comb her hair, and she looked as though she had just woken up, rolled over, and hopped on the bus for school. Was that confidence or laziness?

Candice stayed two houses behind me, so in the mornings my mother had to leave earlier than usual; I'd stop by her house and ride with her and her step brother. That allowed us to gossip and share candid truths about our lives. I was pretty naïve, so I asked Candice lots of questions. Candice taught me many things, and some of her explanations left me queasy. How she came to learn all of this at that young age is beyond me, especially when she began those awful talks about sex! She explained in intricate detail about a dog position, and I almost barfed. As time went on, I learned that she had acquired this knowledge from firsthand experience.

"My step brother taught me," she said. Candice and her step brother had been having sex way before their parents got married and moved in together.

"So, you just freely give your step brother your coochie? Isn't that like against the law or something?" I asked.

"No, silly! We are not blood-related, so it's okay," she assured me.

While I was shooting around with Candice one day, she told me to look at a young man walking onto the courts. A shirtless boy entered the gym, and my jaw dropped.

"Damn Tabby, don't drool all over the court! I don't want you to slip once I bust your ass in this quick game of pickup!" she laughed.

"First of all, you'll never bust my ass in anything. And a girl can look! Who is that Candy? He is fine!" I said to her.

"That's Montel Romero! You don't know who he is? That is one of the Varsity football players! He's a junior!" she said as I tried to gain back my composure.

"Wow! He's beautiful!" I said as I began to drop down and guard her during our game.

"Yeah, he is, and you have a boyfriend, remember?" she asked me.

"Not anymore, he is messing around with this sea donkey at high noon looking chick, so I broke up with him. Or maybe he broke up with me," I laughed.

Candice dropped the basketball, and I watched it roll out of bounds as she fell to the floor, holding her stomach from laughing so hard.

"Girl, you're so damn funny! We surely will miss you on the road games telling all of those jokes," she said.

"You might as well just join the team as much as you are here with us at practice. You shouldn't just give up on your dreams like that," Candice said.

I ignored her.

Yes, I was a staple at practice, and the coach even used me to fill in for drills, but I was content just observing. Watching people play basketball was so therapeutic for me, and I could feel endorphins being released as I watched.

Comedy helped me push through the pain I was feeling. *If I could just laugh it out, and if tears would form from someone's amusement of my misfortune, then it was my escape for a moment.*

"Get up!" I said as we continued to laugh even harder.

We kept playing our game of twenty-one pickup and enjoying each other. I had brushed off the fact with my boyish figure that Montel was even in the room with us. I did glance over my shoulder a few times to see what he was doing, seemingly conditioning his athletic physique as he stretched out on the floor.

Montel was two shades lighter than me with high jawbones and a low hair cut rippling with waves. Montel was shorter than I preferred, but he could get a pass if he knew I existed. With his pointy nose and pink lips, he was just what I liked. I was getting seasick from looking at him across the room.

Korey G. was fine, but Montel was my type. Even though I had not verbally expressed interest in boys over the years, I had eyes in my head, and I would always admire them from afar.

"What's up with a little one-on-one?" I heard a male voice echo from behind me. The gym floor shook as the steps grew heavier and closer. That voice stopped just behind me. Candice stopped dead in her tracks, and now her jaw dropped in awe of this godly man.

"He's talking to you, Tabby!" Candice whispered as she pointed in Montel's direction.

I stayed in my squatting defense position and turned my upper body towards him.

"Hi," I said in a mousy voice, and in that awkward position, I lost my balance and fell on the floor.

"Great!" Candice mouthed as she slapped her face in embarrassment for me.

I kept my eyes to the floor, afraid to see his reaction to my clumsy spill.

"Hey," said Montel sheepishly as he walked over and reached out his left hand to help me up. "I'm Montel. What's your name?" he asked.

I looked up and reached my hand up to connect with his. I was shocked that Montel was even talking to me.

"My name is Tabitha," I finally said very slowly.

"Nice to meet you, Tabitha. I've seen you around school..." he trailed off as he rubbed the back of his firm neck.

What school did he go to? I thought to myself in absolute confusion.

I don't remember seeing him around, and I wondered why he would even recognize me or notice me. Was it because I was goofy? Was this some kind of prank?

"Oh, really?" I was treading carefully.

"Make-up, weave, stiff hair, or those tight-fitting clothes. You stand out against all that nonsense," he said.

I was taken aback because all these other guys who would pucker their faces up in disgust at the sight of me, and this one over here was expressing admiration. I guess he had a type, just like I did. I was glad to know that I was his type, as well.

"Is it okay if I call you sometime? I have to get to football practice right now," Montel said.

"Sure," I said and recited my number.

"One second," he said as he reached into his workout bag and grabbed an ink pen.

I wondered if he did this all the time. I mean, who kept a pen in their workout bag?

"Tabitha? Did you hear me?" he said as he attempted to make eye contact with me.

"Oh! I am so sorry! It's 919-555-2288," I repeated.

"Okay, I will call you tonight!" He grabbed his bag and ran out of the gym.

I watched him dash off, his shoulders glistening and noticed he was standing just a bit taller than when he entered.

"Yes, girl! I am not sure what he wants with you, but it doesn't even matter! That brother is fine!" Candice said.

Even my friend didn't have faith in me.

We finished our game of twenty-one pick up and headed outside to wait for someone to pick me up. It was typically my mother, who was typically late. But since Saul and Barak had cars now, one of them would come if they weren't working.

They were lucky to have vehicles, but it wasn't unusual for other high school kids to have their own cars. My brothers inherited their cars from someone in the family. Saul's car came from one of our cousins, Jack. He was allegedly some big-time drug dealer in Durham, and he was on top of the world until three men broke into his home, tied him up, and robbed him of everything, including six bricks of raw cocaine and over $100,000 in cash. But that was not all the robbers did! They also pistol-whipped Jack and sodomized him several times. I'd never heard of such a story. But then again, this was the age of learning all things taboo or maybe just one of the ailments of the 90's.

Jack ended up losing his mind. He began to get high off his own supply. Jack already had a personal coke habit that most successful drug dealers had as they became a product of their environment. But this time, he became homeless and started smoking crack-cocaine. Jack couldn't bounce back from his traumatic experience. And that's how Saul got his charcoal grey 1992 Nissan 300ZX. My grandmother was married to Jack's grandfather, so his mother was my grandmother's daughter-in-law. My grandmother was still running her liquor houses at night, and she had money to throw around. So, she purchased it for Saul.

Barak's car wasn't as fancy. My great, great grandfather left a 1988 burgundy Oldsmobile Delta behind when he passed, and my grandmother gave it to Barak. Fortunately, Barak was not into flashy cars, so he grew to love this colossal car and named it "Flight 88.

Chapter 10: Let Her Go

To my surprise, my mother was waiting for me outside of school.

"How was school?" My mother stood in front of her car with her arms crossed, staring me down as I walked across the yard.

"It was...cool?" I responded, pausing with wonder at her surprise appearance.

Since my brothers dropped out, my mother took great interest in what was happening with me in school. There was complete silence in the car, and there were moments where I wanted her just to ask me how I felt about Korey G., about being a teenager, about love and what it really meant. But she never did. I was still hurting on the inside and felt the solution was to date someone else to help me get over Korey G. It felt as if we were really done, so if Montel called, I was going to go for it.

After I took a shower and laid back to relax on my daybed, my phone rang.

"Hello?"

"Tabby? Is this you?" a sweet masculine voice asked.

This sure wasn't Korey G.

After I found out about Korey and Tiara and having my phone off the hook for a few days, surely he realized that it was over. I didn't even know if he had tried to call me. Due to my inexperience, it never occurred to me to have a conversation with Korey G. and just be straight up with him about this not working for us. So, I opted to move on.

"Is this Montel?" I asked and giggled.

"Yes! Is it okay to call you, Tabby?" he asked.

Okay? This was perfect timing. I wanted to tell him that he could call me whatever he wanted, but I didn't want to come off as desperate. I thought of all types of ways to respond to him. I could hear Candice telling me to make my voice sound "sexy." But I just decided to be myself.

"Sure, I guess. How was football practice?" I asked.

We talked on the phone for hours and caught up on life, and he gave me the history of his parents. He never knew his father, because he was incarcerated. Montel resided with his mother and younger brother forty-five minutes away from our high school. He told me how he got into football, and we exchanged notes on sports. We truly had a lot in common, and I was happy to get to know him.

"So, what made you ask me for my number? That doesn't happen often. I want to know why." I asked Montel.

Just then, I heard someone else on the line. Either it was my brothers attempting to dial out on my private line, or it was someone on his end.

There was silence, and then I spoke.

"Hello?" I said.

"Montel! It's ten o'clock! If you don't get off the phone with these little fast-ass girls!" an older woman yelled, knowing I could hear.

Suddenly, I heard a dial tone. I was all alone once again.

Did he just hang up on me? I hope that it was out of pure embarrassment. He could have told me he would talk to me later, or he would see me at school, or something.

I hung up and laid there. I didn't know what to think. Maybe this wasn't the guy for me because clearly, his mother was going to be a pain.

And how dare she call me a fast-ass? She knew nothing about me. She must have been a case of a bitter single mother, especially since he said that neither one of his younger brothers had their dads around. I was quick to judge her. If only I knew how wrong I was.

I couldn't imagine being a single mother raising two boys alone. Money was probably tight for them, and his mother may have been tired and angry because she didn't have help. Her son, Montel, was so fine that girls probably called the house chasing him down all the time. So, as a single mother, she was probably worried that he would get a girl pregnant. And that would cause her even more burden that she could simply afford.

But that is me, the now mature narrator who knows what it is to be a single mother.

Yet in that moment, when I had such little info about life and was still learning about the birds and the bees. I needed to ask Candice why his mother was so tense. How could it be that simply talking to a boy could mean pregnancy? Only Candice could tell me. I wondered why she knew so much more than me. Was her mother giving her this information? Because my mother wasn't having any of these coming of age stories with me.

Montel's mother was intercepting my groove with her son, and it wasn't cool. My mother never did anything like that; she would just take my phone away. I had a little bit more freedom than Montel, that was for damn sure.

I told Saul I'd see him later and hopped out of the car and hit a light jog to get to Montel, who was waiting outside for me.

"I'm sorry," he immediately blurted out.

"Your mother was tripping last night! You don't have your own line?" I asked.

"My own line? We can't afford that. Do you have your own line?" Montel asked.

"Duh! Yes! My mother lets me have whatever I want!" I told him.

"You're lucky!" Montel said and held the doors open for me.

As we approached the lobby, the first bell rang for us to be in class.

"I'll see you later. Lunch?" Montel asked.

"Of course," I said, and we hugged, then parted ways to our classes. I felt butterflies flutter within me and whisked me away until lunch.

I was excited to have someone showing me some attention, even though it had only been days since I released Korey G. from my mind. I went to class and tried to focus on the lesson that my teacher was discussing, but I couldn't. All I could think about was how life was before I started engaging with people of the opposite sex. Now it seemed like these boys consumed my thoughts and a large chunk of my still-developing mind!

We had block schedules that consisted of "A" days and "B" days. Both days pretty much looked the same, but you had four classes on "A" days, two in the morning and two in the afternoon. The classes were each one-and-a-half hours. In between the first two, we had lunch, which lasted an entire hour. We had a soul food line, an Italian line, a taco line, regular school lunch, and then a Domino's pizza cart by the auditorium that sold by the slice. The kids who drove would go out and grab fast food. The rest of us hung around the lobby near the cafeteria and gossiped, gave each other side looks, and shook with laughter.

I refused to eat school lunch. It always looked creepy and slimy to me, and when you came from a household where your mother could "throw down" in the kitchen, you weren't trying to eat frozen chicken nuggets, the rectangular frozen pizza, and stale corn for lunch. I was somewhat of a picky eater and had a thing about textures, so I opted out.

I got behind a line of ten people at the pizza cart when I felt someone's body heat behind me, someone was entirely too close, but I didn't turn around to see who it was. It felt threatening. Then I felt two arms wrap around my waist, and I instantly tensed up.

"I missed you," he said in my ear.

I tried to turn around, but strong male arms had me in a tight grip so that I couldn't turn either way. I lifted my hand to touch the person's face, and as soon as I stroked the jawline, I knew who it was.

"I missed you more," I said once I realized it was Montel.

I turned around and gave him the biggest hug, and for a moment, I forgot that we were in school. I began to feel hot all over, and it was a feeling I had not had before.

"Pizza, huh?" he said.

"Sure, you want some?" I asked him.

"Nah, I'm good. I'll just grab a tray from the regular lunch line," he said.

I paused for a second. Here I was with my fancy phone line, my cash for lunch, and Montel was totally okay with doing without.

"It's okay, I have extra money if you'd like some," I insisted.

Montel paused and examined his pride.

"Pepperoni, okay?" I asked as I turned to order.

"Can I have four slices of pepperoni, please?" I asked.

The slices went for two dollars apiece, so I handed over my twenty as Montel grabbed the warm slices.

"We can get some sodas from the drink machine," I said.

Montel just nodded. He could tell that I was assertive and very domineering, so he just went along with the plan.

"Thank you," he said as we walked towards the vending machine.

"It's my pleasure," I said to him.

"So, I guess this is our first date?" he asked me.

"Really? I guess so," I said, smiling from ear-to-ear.

I put one dollar into the drink machine and looked at Montel to see what beverage he wanted. He looked more like a Coca-Cola guy than anything, and I was right.

"I'm okay with a Coke," he smiled.

His smile was illuminating.

I grabbed our drinks, and we found an empty bench in the hallway by the cafeteria. The seniors always took these, but I guess they were ours today. We sat on the bench and laughed and talked. Montel said he had a home game this Saturday, and he wanted me to come.

"I'm flattered," I smiled.

"I would love to see that beautiful face in the stands when I glance out. Please tell me you'll come," he pleaded.

"I wouldn't miss it for the world," I told him.

As we sat and ate, some of Montel's teammates walked up to us. Montel gave them a pound and asked them if they were ready for the game on Saturday. They made small talk while I ate my pizza. They never acknowledged me.

Then, one of his teammates looked at me.

"Bro, who is this? She looks like one of us," he said, as he and the other teammates started laughing.

Montel stood up from the bench, dropping his pizza.

"Bro! What is that about? This is a friend of mine! Not cool!" he responded.

"My bad bro, I just expected you to have more of an exotic type," he said with a sullen look on his face. He was genuinely confused.

"Bro, your time here is up!" Montel said as he walked closer into his teammate's face.

They stared eye-to-eye for ten seconds before I intercepted.

"Montel. It's okay," I said and grabbed his hand.

His teammates threw their hands up and walked away after realizing Montel didn't find their jokes funny at all.

He sat back down beside me and placed his hands on his head.

"I'm sorry about that," he said.

"Seriously, it's okay. I get that all the time from the guys here. They think I'm pretty gross because I'm a tomboy," I told him.

"It doesn't matter! I like you, and I want you around so the hell with what everyone else thinks," he said.

I smiled and rubbed the back of his head in an attempt to calm him.

He looked over at me and gazed into my eyes, "I really like you, and I don't care what anyone says about you."

"I believe you. Now let us eat please! We only have twenty minutes before the bell rings."

I picked up his slice of pizza on his plate and started to feed it to him. As we laughed and smiled at each other in the lobby, I felt eyes on us.

Candice told me that everyone wanted Montel, but he wasn't into girls that were fast, well-known, or had been with any of his teammates. So that basically ruled out most of the popular girls in school.

He knew what he wanted, and apparently it was me.

We finished our lunch, and Montel grabbed the trash, dunked it in the bin, and began to walk with me to my next class, Home Economics. That was one of my favorite classes because we spent the entire hour-and-a-half going over recipes, and we baked at least once a week. We were all on teams of three, and everyone picked a recipe. We prepared meals and had a potluck-style luncheon on Fridays.

"I'll see you later," Montel said as we arrived at my class.

"I hope so!" I gave him another hug, and my right leg lifted like it did in the movies when a couple kissed for the first time. As I was turning to walk into class, I saw Shea watching us from down the hall.

"Hi Shea," I waved at her and walked into class. I don't know if she waved back, but I did notice how she looked at me, which I found odd. If she had plans to tell Korey G., well, he was the one cheating on me. Now he was free, and I was moving on.

Montel and I continued to talk on the phone late into the night. We even arranged to act as if we were ending our calls at ten o'clock, and when his nosey mama went back to sleep, he'd call me back. Between seeing each other at school, eating lunch together and spending every night on the phone over three weeks, I realized I really liked him. A lot had transpired between us in a short amount of time.

Montel mentioned to me that he had a big game coming up over the weekend, and he wanted me to be there. They were playing against our rival school. I heard all the hype about it from my teammates, but I wasn't a big football fan. Sure, I went to Montel's games, but I didn't have a clue what was going on while they were on the field. It didn't make sense to me that they blew the whistle that much.

"I know you're going to the rival game this weekend!" Candice said to me since she knew Montel and I had been going strong for weeks now.

"He just asked me yesterday about coming," I told her.

"Good! So, the game is Friday night and a couple of the basketball girls and I are going, and then everyone is going to crash at my place for the weekend! You down to come?" Candice asked.

I began to wonder if I should tell my parents about Montel, or at least let my mother know. Hell, I barely ever saw my step dad because he lived at that restaurant. Besides, he wasn't interested in any aspect of my teenage life. I was on my own. I saw how consistent he was with my mother, but he was not the male role model that I hoped would teach me, speak to me, or share with me so that I can seek that same goodness in a man one day.

My mother didn't tolerate my brothers and me spending the night at other people's houses, so I paused for a second to think. Her stepbrother came to mind, but Candice only lived two houses behind me, so maybe it was okay. We knew better than to ask my mother because she had already made it clear that it was unacceptable. It was Tuesday, so I didn't have much time to procrastinate. I had to ask her ASAP.

Luckily, my mother was picking me up that day, so I was going to ask her on the way home. As soon as she pulled up into the carpool after school, I made sure I was extra nice.

"Hi, mom!" I said as I threw my book bag in the backseat and plopped down in the car.

My mother looked like she was wondering what happened to her little girl that had been so unhappy for the last few weeks. I wasn't surprised that she looked at me that way because right before Korey G. and I broke up, I was very hateful and irritated with everyone. All of the rumors I was hearing about him and Tiara were wreaking havoc with my emotions. I knew he was lying to me about seeing her, so I had an attitude with the entire world.

"Why are you being so nice? What do you want?" my mother inquired.

"So, mom. There's this football game Friday night, and I was wondering if I could go! Also, can I stay at Candice's house afterward? Her mother is going to pick a few of the other girls and us up and let us stay - you know, order pizza and stuff," I explained.

My mother was silent for about a minute or so.

I wondered what she was thinking about as we drove home in silent contemplation. It wasn't like she didn't know Candice and her mother. Candice and I had been playing basketball together for years. Her family was one of the first families we met when we moved up here.

"Mom?" I said.

"I don't think that's a good idea. Candice and her brother are way more advanced than you are," she explained.

"What do you mean, mom? Advanced?"

I wondered what my mother was talking about. Was she alluding to Candice and her step brother having sex? If so, how did she know that? I never told her. My mother would say weird things like this from time-to-time, but she would be accurate. She felt things.

"And football? What do you know about football?" my mother asked me.

"So I have to know about football to attend a game with the other girls? I don't even play basketball anymore, and that was the only thing I had to keep me occupied for a while. Now, I can't even go to an event at my school?" I asked my mother.

"I never said you couldn't go to the game; my concern is you staying over Candice's house with that step brother," she said.

"Mom! What do you think is going to happen?" I asked her.

"I don't know, but I know Candice's mother and her husband have gone out of town a lot, leaving them two alone. I would have to talk to Candice's mother first, in person, before I could make a decision," she responded.

"Oh, my God!" I said as I pouted and slumped in my seat on the passenger's side.

"You sure do need to call on God! If I cannot talk to Candice's mother, you are not going. The end," she said, ignoring my tantrum.

I was so frustrated with my mother at this point. Why was she always trying to go the extra mile and do extra stuff like face-to-face interviews with parents? Why did she need to confirm what I already knew about Candice and her step brother not being so innocent and taking advantage of having sex every time their parents were gone? But I wasn't like that. I wished my mother would notice that I wasn't susceptible all the time.

As soon as the car pulled up in the yard, I hopped out and slammed the car door as hard as I could. I was walking so fast, trying to avoid her that I didn't even see someone standing on the front porch until I was already upon it. We had these cement stones leading up to our front porch not only for décor, but to prevent any of us from tracking in mud, dirt, or water when it rained.

My mother was strategic in everything she did, and she didn't play about her carpet being dirty and her house being clean period.

"Hi gorgeous," said a familiar voice. The voice startled me, so I instantly jumped back off the first step as I dropped my book bag in fear.

"How dare you come to my house after weeks with your tail tucked in between your legs. What do you want?"

Korey G. stood up and reached out to me.

"I missed you. I had to see you since you wouldn't take my phone calls," he said.

"That's bullshit! Aren't you dating Tiara?" I yelled.

"Okay, Tabby! Watch your mouth!" my mother yelled as she approached us.

"I have nothing to say to him!" I answered and ran away from the house towards the park.

The park was always my escape! Not only did I find serene peace there, but it also had a basketball court. The only bad thing about it was that it was a twenty-minute walk and a five-minute drive.

"Tabby! Get back here!" My mother repeatedly yelled. Her voice faded the further I ran away.

I was running so hard that I didn't notice the panting and footsteps behind me. All I heard was my heart beating faster and harder, pushing the blood of ancestors and long-gone men who'd left me here to fend on this earth. I ran against concrete and dirt and mud. I ran against the wind that pushed me back to where I came from. I ran against the horizon that always seemed to take a step back every time I asked it to come closer.

After six minutes of hardcore sprinting, my feet came up from under me, torpedoing my body to the ground. Korey G. had hawked me down and pulled me to the ground by my shirt. I rolled over on my back; the blue sky spread above me; its freedom beckoning me while I was pinned to the earth. I balled my hands into tight fists, the only way I knew to defend myself.

"What do you want? Why can't you just leave me alone?" I cried and pleaded as I kicked to make contact with Korey G.'s groin.

"I love you, Tabby!" Korey G. said.

"You call this love? This isn't love!"

Korey G. let go, and I sat up. He started walking in circles with his hands on his temples.

"It's over, Korey G.! I will never be second to anyone! You are just like my father! Manipulative and conniving, and I despise people like you!" I cried.

"Tabby, I'm not your father, and I will never leave you! See, I'm here!" he kneeled down to rub my shoulders.

I nodded in approval with my thoughts. Korey G. wasn't good for me.

"No! No!" I cried.

Korey G.'s grip tightened on my arms.

When I looked at his face, he mirrored a wolf in sheep's clothing.

Through gritted teeth, he said, "So, you think you're just going to dump me and date some football guy at the school, huh?"

Thanks a lot, Shea.

"I won't let it happen! I will kill both of you! You hear me, Tabby?"

Who was this monster?

"Stop it! You're hurting me!" I screamed.

"You will never leave me! You hear me? We will all die first!" he repeated.

At this point, I took stock of my location - all the way at the back of my cul-de-sac, where there wasn't a soul in sight. Korey G. paced back and forth as if he had already killed me and dumped my body in a river in his mind; he just needed to implement his plan.

I was scared for my life and made the split-decision to play along. I composed myself and realized that sometimes *abusers* need assurance.

"Okay, okay! I love you, Korey G.!" I said to make him stop pacing. I stood up, brushed myself off, and grabbed his hand. I was sure to make eye contact with him.

"That's right, baby! It is all or nothing! You and me!" I yelled with passion.

He stopped, searched my eyes, and saw what he was looking for. He began to cry.

"You mean it? You won't leave me? Ever?" he asked.

"I won't. I'm right here," I assured him, and pushed aside how this would bite me in the butt later. I needed to get back to my mom's house.

"Hey, my mother is probably worried about us. Let's head back to the house." I whispered and attempted to pull his hand in the direction of my house.

Korey G. tightened his grip and said, "No! You need to make sure this is what you really want. I have to know how this will end!"

Now, I was seriously worried. I remembered my mother's God and that I could talk to Him.

But not out loud. Silent, in my head.

God. Are you there? I know that I have not always believed in You and I even cracked jokes about You at times. If you are genuine, I need you to come to see me right now. God, I'm sorry for all the bad things I said about You. Please come. Can you even hear me, God? I pray our talks are not in vain!

Korey G., still holding my hand tight, silently stared off into the wooded area behind our subdivision.

"Tabitha! Tabby! Let's go!" I turned around and saw my mother waiting for me to get in her car.

Korey G. instantly dropped my hand, and I took off to my mother's vehicle as fast as I could. Once I got to my mother's car, all of my fear and anxiety surfaced.

"Korey G.! You okay up there? You need a ride?" she asked him.

"Mom, he's cool on the hill. Let's just go!" I said. I squirmed and rubbed the palm of my increasingly sweaty hands.

"Are you okay, Tabby? What is going on?" she asked.

"Mom! Just, please! Pull off!"

My mother hit the gas so hard; I jerked back into the seat.

Thank God she showed up because I didn't recognize this version of Korey G. His eyes looked like the eyes of a feral animal, and I feared for my life. I didn't know why I was going through this type of pressure as a teenager. All I knew was he did me wrong, and I wanted out!

As we pulled up to the house, I wondered what made my mother come looking for me. Maybe her God did exist! Maybe He answered my prayer. Wow! If that was really her God, He was quick to respond! Or maybe it was a coincidence. Either way, I was thankful.

I ignored my mother's attempts to talk to me and locked myself in my bedroom as soon as we got home. I laid there thinking about my next move. Here I was trying to move on, and now Korey G. wants to try and weasel his way back into my life after having an affair. I had trusted him, and he was the first boy I ever loved, and he betrayed me.

Two soft knocks at my door roused me from my thoughts.

"You want to talk about it?" my mother asked me tentatively as she sat down beside me.

"Not really," I said as I slammed my pillow on my face.

"I'm concerned," my mother asked.

"Mom, Korey G. is not who you think he is," I said to her.

"What do you mean? He's just hurt because he thinks you've moved on," she said.

"I did, mom, just like he did with the girl around the corner," I yelled.

"He's not dealing with that girl, Tabby; he just helps her out with rides to and from work. You know she's a single mother and has that little girl to care for," she explained.

"I don't care about any single mother being in need. Korey G. was my boyfriend. Besides, that's his sister's friend. Korey G. has you fooled, mom. He's definitely not a saint!"

"You guys need to work through this," my mother said.

At this point, I got quiet and didn't tell her that he just threatened me because she wouldn't believe me.

"Get out!" I yelled.

My mother stared at me for a few seconds and then stood over me.

"Remember, I'm still your mother, so watch your mouth," she said as she left.

"Ugh!" I yelled and threw my pillow as hard as I could at my door.

My mother didn't get it at all. She had only been with two men her entire life, and she married both, so what did she know about boyfriend issues? Sometimes she was impossible. I didn't know why my mother was solely on Korey G's side. But, there wasn't anything he could tell me about why he was hanging at Tiara's house that I was going to buy. I still had to make the Friday football game and sleepover at Candice's happen.

I asked my oldest brother Saul to drop me off at school the next morning on his way to work. Montel was waiting for me at the blue doors, just like always. Montel instantly detected something was wrong. He wrapped his arms around me and the feeling of warmth and security broke down my defenses, and I began to weep.

Montel held me tighter.

It was at that moment that I realized all I needed was a hug to let me know that everything was going to be alright. My life seemed way more peaceful before this "boyfriend stuff."

"I'm not sure if I can see you anymore," I told him.

"What do you mean? Is that why you didn't take my calls last night?" Montel let go of me.

"No, Montel! I forgot to turn my ringer back on. I would never intentionally ignore your calls," I cried.

"Tell me what's going on," he said as the first bell rang.

"Can we talk during lunch? I just need some time to process my thoughts," I said to him.

"Okay," he said as he rubbed my shoulders.

Montel walked me to my first class and waited until I was at my desk. He waved and jogged off. He was a star athlete so he couldn't be late for classes and his grades had to be above a passing average. His coach claimed he didn't coach dumb athletes. "It's a package deal!" Montel would say, as he mocked his coach when he talked to the football team about grades and talent going hand-in-hand.

When class started, I doodled my thoughts about my life. I wrote the word "escape" and put it in quotation marks with several boxes around it. And then it hit me; I need an escape to get to the game on Friday night. Maybe I could tell my mother that they were going to have basketball tryouts again. Or, maybe I could say to her I was helping with the food drive that my home economics teacher had planned. But it had to be realistic since my mother knew the game was on Friday.

"Arthur! Get out of my classroom. I'm writing you up for detention!" Mrs. Magnum yelled.

I forgot about my escape plan as Arthur performed one of his many stunts. Arthur was the class clown and was always getting into trouble. Usually, Mrs. Mangum would warn him several times before sending him out. But whatever he had done this time must have pissed her off. Or she was just having a bad day. Nevertheless, she sent him out of her class. The whole class moaned and laughed at Arthur as he danced his way out of our classroom. Arthur was exceedingly comical in anything he did, but there is a time and place for everything.

I shook my head at Arthur as he left the classroom, and I returned to doodling. This time I wrote the thought that was on the forefront of my mind and that was the word "trouble." I circled it a few times, and then another lightbulb went off. My mind raced, and my genius superpowers kicked in. I could tell my mother that I got in trouble at school today, and I have detention on Friday! That was perfect. My mother would ground me by taking my landline phone and not allow me to leave the house for a few days, but it was totally going to be worth it. I would stay after school, serve my detention, help with the food drive, and have Saul pick me up after work at nine o'clock. I got excited thinking about going to my first football game with my friends and my new boo, Montel.

Lunchtime came around, and I saw Montel in the café lobby talking to some girl I had never seen her before, so I walked up fast and threw myself in-between them.

"Oh! Hey, Tabby!" he said, smiling from ear-to-ear.

"Hi," I said, blushing back at him, giving him the biggest hug ever.

"This is my best friend, Tanika. Tanika, this is the girl I was telling you about," he said.

I reached my hand out to shake hers, but she never lifted her hand and gave Montel the look of death.

"I'll talk to you later!" she said as she walked off, looking at me over her shoulders.

"Okay! If I had not known any better, I would think she had a thing for you!" I said to him.

"Who? Tanika? No way! She's just very territorial," he laughed.

"Right," I said as I tried to fight off the frustrations of her being rude.

"Don't worry about her. She just has issues with anyone new because she's seen what girls have done to me in the past. But enough about her, what was on your mind from this morning?" he asked.

I paused for a second and processed what Montel had just said about previous girls doing him wrong, and I opted not to tell him about Korey G.

"Nothing Montel, it's not important! Let's get some pizza!" I said to him as I brushed him off.

"Are you sure?" he asked me to sound concerned.

"I'm positive, Montel, let's eat," I said, cracking a fake smile.

Deep down, I wasn't okay. I needed him to interrogate me until I told him what was wrong. My mother taught me that a man who pays attention to you loves you.

Instead, Montel grabbed my hand and led me over to the pizza stand. I acted as if everything was fine. I didn't want Montel to catch wind that my ex-boyfriend didn't know he was my ex and that he was a lunatic. It scared me in regard to how close Montel and I were getting in such a short period of time. I really liked him, but he was a rebound crush, and I was starting to think maybe this wasn't fair to him.

"Are you coming to my game Friday?" he asked.

"Yes!"

"I can't wait to see you in the bleachers cheering me on. I have something for you," he said and unzipped his book bag.

When I saw what he pulled out, I gasped. Montel had an extra jersey with the number five on it, and he wanted me to wear it to his game to represent him.

"Oh my God! Are you serious? You really want me to wear this?" I asked him. Then my insecurities kicked in. Out of all the beautiful girly girls in the school, he picked me. I was honored and in awe at the same time.

"I can't wait to wear your jersey, Montel!"

He smiled from ear-to-ear as he gobbled down the rest of his pepperoni slice.

As I headed back to class, I decided to put my plan in motion when my mother picked me up today from school. I was going to act like I was sad and frustrated that I got in trouble in school and gauge her reaction.

When the final bell rang, I rushed through school to the carpool line. My mother was the second car that had pulled up, so she was possibly in a good mood because that meant she got off early. I put on my serious demeanor. I threw my book bag in the backseat and pouted, folded my arms, and stared out the window.

"You have a good day at school?" my mother asked me.

"Not really! I got in trouble today in my second-period class," I said under my breath.

"Trouble? What do you mean you got in trouble?" she asked as she pulled over behind the school building. I always wondered why my mother pulled over as if the news I had to tell her would make a difference if she were driving or sitting still.

"I was talking in class, mom, and the teacher asked me twice to stop talking, and I didn't. So, she said I had two days of detention starting tomorrow and Friday," I said as I rolled my eyes.

My mother didn't say anything immediately; she resumed driving the car while she shook her head. Her silence was going to be long and awkward for the twenty-minute ride home.

Then she spoke, "So what are you trying to do? You want to end up like your brothers as high school dropouts and working a minimum-wage job?"

I wasn't happy with that comparison since I was still in school and had particularly good grades. So, what if I didn't play basketball and end up getting a full ride to GSU? I was still attending school. I felt like my mother was silently angry because I gave up basketball. But it was solely my decision at the end of the day, and no one could make me play basketball if I didn't want to.

"I'm nothing like them."

"And I'm surprised that school didn't call me. They call me for everything else," my mother said.

Good point. I surely wasn't going to respond to that.

When we got to the house, I hurried inside to avoid my mother, which was the plan until I got through the next few days. I didn't even come out of my room for dinner. Instead, I daydreamed about being an adult. I thought how awesome it would be to come and go as you please without someone breathing down your neck all the time. I wasn't about to get on the phone with Montel after practice because if my mother caught me, she was going to trip.

The next day was my first day of fake detention, which meant I'd be at school until 7 pm. I had already planned that I would just sit at Montel's practice and attempt to learn what playing football entailed.

Montel and I went through our routine of him walking me to my first class, eating lunch together, and blowing each other kisses throughout the day. When the last bell of the day rang, I went to look for Candice before she started practice to tell her that I would indeed be at the football game that night.

"Hey girl," I said as I found Candice warming up for practice.

She usually had the same routine every day, and I always knew where to find her.

"Really?" she asked.

"Yes! So, I guess I will just wait for you after practice, and then we can walk up to the field together," I said.

"Sure! That sounds like a plan! You sure you don't want to stay and shoot around?" Candice asked.

"No, thank you, I'm good," I said as I walked off the court.

I headed out to the football field to watch Montel's practice. I guess I was a little bit early because none of the players were on the field yet. While I waited, I looked through my book bag and grabbed one of my new notebooks. I felt like I needed to write down my thoughts, especially since the incident with Korey G. transpired days ago, though I had not heard from him in days. I guess that was a good thing. Even if he were calling, my mother wouldn't tell me because she knew I was over that entire situation.

Before I could get a full page of the thoughts running rampant in my head, I heard thundering footsteps and yelling. The Varsity football team ran out to the field. I guess it was their thing to yell to get themselves hyped and energized before a game.

Intrigued by their synchronized running, I put my notebook aside and focused on what the team was getting ready to do. I watched the team run plays, something I was familiar with from basketball.

I got bored after a while but didn't want to walk off because Montel was super-excited to have his "girl" support him at football practice, and I was determined not to let him down. At least Candice and two of her friends would be with me tomorrow to keep me company. I was glad Barak was picking me up because I didn't want to have to fake being frustrated about detention again. It surprised me that my mother didn't follow up with the school about my detention. She may have been burned out about school matters because of my brothers.

I couldn't wait for Montel to come out after practice because I had to make sure I was there when Barak pulled up. He always snitched on me, so I was relentlessly one step ahead. Just as I got there, Barak yelled out the passenger window.

"Tabb-bb-bb! Come on!" he said.

He sounded frustrated and rushed. I hopped in and said, "How was your day, bro?"

"The same," he responded.

"The same as what?" I asked him.

"You look mighty bubbly for someone who just got out of detention," Barak smirked.

"Huh? Am I supposed to be sad? At least *I'm* still in school!"

I must have struck a nerve because Barak was quiet the whole way home. Saul and Barak dished it out all the time, but they couldn't handle the same from me. Nevertheless, I wasn't going to get consumed with his misery. Sometimes I felt as though Barak hated his life because he quit school and didn't get to continue playing basketball. But between his struggles with dyslexia and his poor grades, he figured not only was he wasting his time, but it was futile for the teacher as well.

I was ready to shower and wait on Montel's call. I busted through the front door and was rushing to my room when my mother said, "Tabitha! We need to talk, please."

The tempting smell of pepper steak smothered in gravy with green peppers and onions hung in the air, but it wasn't enough to lure me into opening up to my mother.

"I'll be right back; I need to drop my bags in my room!"

"I said, come here *now*, and that's what I mean!" my mother yelled.

She sounded serious, so I made a U-turn and bee lined it to the kitchen.

"Yes, mom, what's up?" I asked.

"Are you aware that Korey G. has been calling here every day, crying and asking for me to talk you into being back with him? He says that you're dating a football player at the school now, and you don't want him because he dropped out of school?"

"Mom, the fact that he dropped out of school has nothing to do with why I don't want to deal with him anymore. Remember that day when we were at the bottom of the cul-de-sac? He threatened to kill me, mom. I think Korey G. is dangerous, and I don't have the energy anymore to entertain him. He chose to be with Tiara around the corner," I said and then added sarcastically, "I wish them well."

"I don't know what's going on, but if you're truly ending it with him, give him an explanation so he can stop worrying me," she said as she stirred the food.

When I got back to my room, I picked up the phone to call Korey G., then decided not to. I didn't care what my mother thought I should do with Korey G., and I didn't owe him an explanation. Hell, he didn't give me one when he moved on with the woman that was practically my neighbor.

I knew that Shea was reporting to Korey G. about Montel and me because she always crept around lunchtime to see what we were doing. I'd catch her staring at us. Why did she care what I was doing when Korey G. was dating her cousin now?

So, I waited for Montel's call as I laid his jersey across my bed and realized I couldn't wear it out of the house in the morning. I'd throw it in my book bag and hope that it wouldn't get too wrinkled. I took a shower and answered Montel's call.

"How are you?" Montel asked.

I know he could hear me smiling through the phone.

"Better now," I said.

We talked about his football game and how excited he was. He was so passionate about sports just like I was, so it was refreshing to date someone that got the same high you did when recollecting sports.

"So, I've been thinking. I know it's only been a few weeks, but would you be my girl? Sorry, it's not more formal with a letter with all of the boxes you must check. I just couldn't wait until tomorrow," he said.

"Yes! The answer is yes!" I screamed.

I must have been too loud because I heard my mother scream for me to go to bed from the living room.

I ignored her.

"You've made me the happiest girl in the world!" I whispered.

"I'm happy too. I talked to my mother about it tonight on the ride home from practice, and she wants to meet you. So maybe I can introduce you two after the game tomorrow," he said.

As happy as I was that he offered to let me meet his mother, I wondered how I was going to pull it off because I told my mother and brother that detention was over at 7 pm. The lies were catching up with me, and I was in too deep at this point. Nevertheless, I was going to figure it out later and enjoy the moment.

After a while, Montel and I got sleepy.

"I'll see you tomorrow. I can't wait to see you in my jersey," he said.

"You're not the only one. Goodnight."

I was finally happy. I didn't get love from any men in my life, so I was thankful for Montel, the second person of the opposite sex that showed me, love.

I finally dozed off, anticipating the rising of the sun.

The next morning, I couldn't wait to get to school. I was up way earlier than normal. I even brushed my hair back into a bun and tucked away loose, straggly strands. I packed Montel's jersey in my bag and went out to the living room.

"Who's taking me to school?" I yelled.

Silence. I stormed in the direction of my mother's room. I knocked excessively hard and sighed loudly.

"Ma!" I yelled.

"What is it, Tabby?" she yelled back.

"So, I guess I'm just not going to school today, huh?" I asked.

My mother must have had the day off because she was clearly indulging in some good sleep.

More silence.

I had to take matters into my own hand. I wondered if Candice and her mother left for school yet. I darted out of the front door in a hurry. I didn't even realize I didn't get lunch money from my step dad until I was already halfway behind my house, attempting to catch Candice. Since she lived directly behind me, it was going to be easy for me to catch them. Normally, Candice and her brother got to school about the same time as me in the morning, so they probably hadn't left yet. I turned the corner so fast in-between houses, it felt as though I twisted my ankle. As I got closer to Candice's house, I saw her mother's red Nissan Altima in the driveway with smoke coming from the pipe. They must have already started the car and were preparing to leave shortly. I ran up the five steps to her house, and to my surprise, the front door was open. Candice was sitting on the couch with her book bag strapped to her back, headphones on, and bobbing her head back and forth. I felt a wave of relief that made me smile internally as I knocked on the glass screen door.

Candice jumped up off the couch to open the door.

"Hey Tabby!" she said as she unlocked the screen door and opened it to let me in.

"Hey, girl!" I said as I walked into her house and sat down beside her.

"What's up? You need a ride to school?" she asked.

It was refreshing to have a friend that knew what I needed without me even speaking.

"Actually, I do. I think my mother overslept," I laughed.

"Listen, I know your mother is really strict when it comes to you. But you should ask her if you could ride with us daily. I'm sure my mother wouldn't mind," she offered.

"Really? You know mom dukes do be tripping, but I'm going to ask her this evening when I get home," I told her.

In my mind, I thought that was ideal, but my mother was so overprotective that she probably wouldn't agree with it.

We got in the car a few moments later.

"So, your mom actually let you go to the game... or did she?" Candice asked me with a smirk on her face.

"She did, in a way, I guess. She thinks I'm in detention," I said as I bit my bottom lip. I bit my bottom lip whenever I was overthinking out loud.

Candice shook her head and laughed. "Well, I'm happy you're coming, but if your mom finds out you lied, she won't be so happy," she said and made eye contact with me.

Candice was right. However, my mother would have never let me go to the football game without me fabricating something, so that is what I did. I felt bad, but the fact that I didn't have to face her this morning made it a little bit easier.

I watched Candice bop her head the entire way to school. She was a true athlete at heart just like I was, and listening to music is how she prepped for her day. I was also a thinker, so I stared out the window at the green country scenery, thinking about if I got caught in this lie I had conjured up. Plus, my mother was off today, so she was possibly going to be preoccupied with paying bills and such. That was also the time that she and my step dad spent together since he worked so much. Friday was his busiest day at the pizza parlor, so he would typically leave late in the afternoon and close the restaurant at midnight.

As we got closer to the school, I unzipped my book bag and threw on the jersey Montel had given me over my white t-shirt.

Candice rested her chin on her hand, rocked back and forth, and said, "Oh, you guys must be official now!"

"Yes, we are," I said as I smiled back at her.

"Those girls are going to be mad at you. Especially Montel's bestie!" she laughed.

"Good! There's something about her I can't put my finger on."

My gut feeling was that Montel's bestie was secretly into him, or were my insecurities raging? Either way, I wasn't buying the whole, "she doesn't like who I date because the previous relationship went sour."

We arrived at school on time, and Montel was waiting for me like he always did. I thanked Candice's mom and rushed to give him a big hug. He kissed me softly on my cheek and wrapped his arm around my shoulders as we headed to my first class.

"I love the jersey on you! Thank you for always supporting me," he said.

"You're welcome," I said and entered my classroom.

"Tabby!" Montel called out. We made eye contact as he stood in the hall. "I love you!" he said.

Oh! Be still my heart! I couldn't believe he told me he loved me. What triggered him to say that? Did I love him? I wasn't sure! Maybe I did. I thought we were taking things slowly. Shouldn't I be more happy than confused?

The rest of class was a blur! All I could think about was how I felt about him, and this puppy love thing we had going on. My classmates stared at me, then turned and whispered to each other. I assumed they were talking about me wearing Montel's jersey. I wasn't worried about it until this girl who sat in front of me and never said two words to me, turned to face me and said, "Isn't number five Montel's jersey?"

"Who wants to know?" I asked.

She just turned back around in her chair, rolled her eyes, and started to giggle with her friends.

By lunchtime, I was irritated by all the pointing and whispering. As I turned the corner, a crowd surrounded the bench where Montel and I ate lunch. It was Montel's teammates in a huddle. They grabbed each other around the shoulders and bounced from side-to-side for a few seconds and then chanted like they did when I watched practice yesterday.

"It's a ritual," Candice said as she walked up behind me.

"Oh, okay. I didn't know what was going on," I said.

"Football players are silly, and they're always hyper. They also do this before every game at lunchtime," she said.

I guess I had been up under a rock because I had never paid attention to it before. Montel peeped his head around his teammates to blow me a kiss. I blushed and followed Candice to the pizza stand.

"Oh snap! Candice, can you get my food today? I didn't have time to ask my step dad for money this morning," I said.

"Sure, Tabby! You know I got you! Pepperoni okay?" she asked.

"Yes, that's fine, and I'll pay you back tomorrow," I assured her.

"Girl, you're good for it. Just get me next time," she smiled.

Just then, I felt the warmth from somebody coming up behind me who covered my eyes with their hands.

"I know it's you, Montel!" I laughed.

"How did you know?" he said as he spun me around to face him.

"Because you're the only person allowed to touch me," I said as I playfully pushed him off me.

"You guys are so cute," Candice handed me my pizza.

We all copped a squat in the corner by the double doors of the lobby to the cafeteria. We caught up on sports, and Candice and Montel educated me about the game of football so that I wouldn't be so lost at the game tonight. In my opinion, football was meaningless. They blew the whistle too much, and some of those tackles would have me ready to square up with someone. The bell rang for us to head to our third class of the day, and we dragged our feet.

"I'll catch up with you guys after school," Candice said as she began a slow jog to get to her class.

Montel kissed my cheek as I departed for my next class.

"I'll see you later! You're looking really good!" he winked at me.

I assumed he was alluding to his jersey. I felt all warm and tingly inside.

When you're watching the clock, time drags on and on. I couldn't wait for the festivities after school today. I could hardly stay focused on my academically gifted English class. As I listened to Mrs. Boykin, I got severely depressed. Yes, I was an extremely gifted kid, but I had to admit that this class was challenging. We basically studied the dictionary. She gave us twenty new words every week that we had to dissect them according to her criteria. Then, we had to write out twenty *verbatim* definitions. There weren't any multiple-choice or matching. So, if you missed one word of the definition, she docked half a point. I didn't understand the logic behind her madness. I mean, where were the literature books for this class? I couldn't believe my counselor opted to put me in here. She stated on my assessment that my middle school teachers repeatedly documented that their curriculum wasn't "challenging enough for me, and I easily got bored." They also mentioned that I doodled during class, didn't study for tests, yet scored one hundred plus on any given test. What they didn't know was my attention span was short, and even though it seemed as if I wasn't listening, I really was. Doodling on paper and writing words was my escape when I had a lot on my mind. Writing and looking at the shapes and curves of letters fascinated me. I always believed this made me unique or maybe even weird.

Then my daydreaming was interrupted.

"Miss Tabitha!" echoed across the room.

"Yes!" I snapped.

"Is everything okay? Do you need to step out in the hall for some fresh air? I mean class did just start, you know," she said sarcastically.

Sometimes these redneck teachers' sarcasm stirred my inner beast, but, this time, I responded with grace.

"What was your question, Mrs. Boykin?" I asked politely and tried not to smirk.

"Define lexicographer, Miss Tabitha," she answered.

The entire class turns around in their seats to look at me.

"Mrs. Boykin, I'm flattered that you gave me such an easy word to define. A lexicographer is a person that makes dictionaries," I said as I stood up and took a bow.

I was thrilled that her attempt to embarrass me in hopes that I didn't know the answer was a big fail. I loved proving people wrong, especially being the only African American female in the classroom.

Mrs. Boykin never addressed the accuracy of my answer but focused more on my bowing. I don't know what was worse, the bow or everyone clapping and laughing for me.

"Miss Tabitha, maybe you should look into being a comedian or sticking to playing basketball rather than attempt to excel in AG classes," she said.

I was appalled that she insulted me, and I had to strike back.

"That's pretty fulsome coming from a midget," I said as I made eye contact with her.

"Get out of my classroom! Now! Go to the principal's office and don't come back," she said and began to shake.

The class laughed hysterically as I grabbed my book bag and left. When I opened the classroom door, I hit the tootsie roll dance to trigger more laughter in my peers, and it worked. The audacity of her to come for me and then when I strike back, now she is appalled. Some people can dish it but cannot take it, I swear.

I walked to the principal's office slowly, not caring what they thought of my actions. I didn't feel any remorse for calling her short. She thought I was out of line as a student, but I thought she was out of line as a teacher. She disrespected me. Here I was, looking crazy because I lied to my mother about having detention, and now, I was possibly about to get it for real. I should have been more careful about what I spoke into existence.

When I walked into the office, Principal Skinner was taking a fax off the machine.

"Ms. Dawson, why are you here? Are you sick because I know star athletes don't get in trouble?" she said.

Principal Skinner was always talking to me in the hallways about basketball and possibly reconsidering joining the basketball team, I'd always brush her off. She stood about five foot three, with short grey hair, and she always wore pearls every time I saw her.

"Principal Skinner, I retired from basketball, and Mrs. Boykin sent me out of her class because she was rude to me, so I reciprocated," I responded flatly.

"Now Ms. Dawson, you know we don't tolerate that behavior. Especially from someone with such a bright future," she said and motioned for me to come into her office.

"Well, Principal Skinner, I assume that you have a teacher in-service about how to address students appropriately. I know you're going to call my mother. Do you want the phone number?" I asked.

"Oh no, I have something better in mind for you, my dear. Instead of detention or investigating why you're in my office, I'm going to ask that you work the concession stand at the football game tonight," she insisted.

"The concession stands. What am I supposed to do? I had planned on watching the football game with my friends," I pleaded with her.

"Nope, one of our volunteers got sick, so instead of bothering your mother at work, I'll just have you help there! Sound fair?" she asked.

"I guess."

I wouldn't even get to sit with my friends at the football game. But I had to consider the upside; Principal Skinner looked out for me because if she had called my mother and explained to her that I had detention, it would have brought heat to myself. Now my little white lie made perfect sense.

"Follow me. You'll spend the rest of the day setting up," Principal Skinner said.

We exited from the gym door and onto the football field to get to the concession stand. It was cool to be skipping Mrs. Boykins's class and hanging with the principal.

As Principal Skinner unlocked the door to the concession stand, I shivered. Football season apparently brought cold weather, and I never wore anything more than a track jacket to school. My mother always fussed that I should wear my "big coat."

"So, Tabitha, all you have to do is start setting up for the game. The popcorn and ice machine must be cut on. It gets busy back here at times, but I'm sure you can handle it," she said with a smile.

I looked around the concession stand and noticed that thing was laid out for the most part. The chips needed to be displayed. The cheese needed to be heated, and the hot dogs needed to be placed in the rack. At this point, I just needed to dive in and figure it out.

"I'll get it done, Principal Skinner! Thank you for not calling my mother and reporting me," I said.

"No worries, my dear. I believe in second chances. I'm heading back to my office; the other volunteers will be here in about an hour," she said.

I prepped the potato chip stand and cut on the popcorn machine to heat up. I turned on the crock pot that held the nacho cheese. I cleaned the counters. My mother taught me that before you start prepping anything food-wise, you need to make sure your area is clean, plus you clean as you go. I applied all my kitchen skills that she had embedded in me thus far, and I got everything up and running.

About an hour later, a parent volunteer showed up. She was a well-dressed Caucasian woman whose perfume brought tears to my eyes.

"You must be Tabitha?" she said with a smile and tucked away her Louis Vuitton purse.

"Yes, ma'am, and I'll be assisting you this evening," I replied.

"Great! It seems as though you know your way around. Have you volunteered here before?" she asked.

"No, ma'am. But I've been here for a while, so I figured it out," I responded.

"That's awesome! By the way. I'm Colt Cyper's mother, number forty-one on the varsity football team. But you can call me Myra," she said with enthusiasm.

I wasn't used to calling adults by their first name, but she insisted.

"Unfortunately, I don't know any of the players personally except Montel. He's my boyfriend," I said with a smile.

"Really? He's a great kid!" she said as she joined me in setting up.

Myra threw on country music via the radio on top of the cooler. She then transitioned into full work mode. An hour passed before I even realized people were starting to arrive to fill the stands. I heard these varsity games got packed quickly, so they were right on time. Principal Skinner said there would be three of us in the concession, but the football team ran out onto the field, and screams arose from the crowd.

"Well, dear, it looks like it'll just be us two this evening, so I hope you got your running shoes on! It's always busy back here!" Myra said.

I scanned the bleachers for a split-second to see if I could locate Candice, but I didn't. She was probably looking for me, but I didn't have a chance to tell her how I ended up behind the concession stand. I was okay with it because football just didn't seem that appealing. Our first customer arrived, a young lady staring at the menu behind me.

"Can I help you?" I asked.

"Sure, can I have a small popcorn and a pop?"

Myra scooped her popcorn while I grabbed a pop from the cooler.

As soon as we completed our first transaction of the evening, we had another customer. I wasn't used to working, and we got busy fast, but Myra helped me maneuver through it.

After a while, I looked up to see Candice watching me.

"Tabitha?" she said and looked confused.

"Oh my God! I if you'd show up here," I said to her.

"What are you doing? I mean, you're working, right?" she asked.

"Long story! I'll tell you tomorrow at the park," I told her. We went to the "park" on Saturday mornings to hoop and shoot around where I'd explain everything to her then.

Candice ordered Skittles, nachos, and a pop, and I sent her on her way. I was thankful she didn't ask too many questions, especially in front of Myra.

I was so busy working; I didn't even realize the football game was coming to an end. I noticed people leaving the football field with two minutes on the clock. The only reason I knew we were winning was that our number was the higher one on the scoreboard.

"Okay, we can start cleaning up now," Myra said and closed and locked the metal shutters. After counting the money, Myra told me I was free to go.

"It was a pleasure working with you, Myra! Thank you for allowing me to assist you!"

"No problem, kiddo! You were the best helper ever, and I'll be requesting you again," she said, smiling.

I hoped she *never* requested me again. Little did Myra know this was a one-time thing because I'd gotten in trouble. That was too much manual labor.

As I headed to the parking lot, it suddenly struck me that I didn't know who was picking me up. Then I saw Montel coming my way, looking past me.

"Montel! What's wrong?" I asked him.

Montel brushed by me quickly without making eye contact.

"Montel! What's wrong with you?" I reached out for him.

He whipped around and said, "Get off me! Stay away from me!" and walked backward for a second until he was out of my reach.

Oh no! He was mad about me not being at the game. Before I could run after him, I heard someone calling my name. I spun around quickly and saw Candice running up the steps towards me.

"Korey G. just pulled a gun on Montel!" she cried.

I grabbed Candice by the shoulders, "Slow down! What happened?"

"I have to check on Montel!" she screamed and ran off.

I was so confused and didn't have a clue what was going on. I looked over at the parking lot and saw my brother's car zooming off. Where was he going? And why was he going so fast through the parking lot? I walked closer to the steps that lead into the parking lot to get a closer perusal on what had possibly just transpired. I ran downstairs to the parking lot in hopes he would turn around, only to watch his taillights grow smaller and smaller as he sped away.

"Can someone please tell me what's going on?" I cried out to the lingering tailgaters.

"I don't know! Someone just pulled a gun on Montel!" One of the rednecks said.

I ran to the payphone and called my mother.

She picked up on the first ring.

"Mom! Can you come to school and get me? Something just happened," I cried, suddenly out of breath.

"Tabby! Please calm down! I can barely understand what you're saying," she pleaded.

"Mom, please come to school and get me! Something awful has happened," I said to her.

"I thought Barack was coming to get you," she said with a disgruntled voice.

"Mom! Please!" I hung up.

I paced back and forth while I waited, trying to piece together what happened. I didn't want to jump to conclusions, but something had gone terribly wrong. Why did Korey G. pull a gun out on Montel? Where did Korey G. even get a gun? Why was he at my school in the first place? Did my brother drive him up here? I finally squatted against a pole and rocked back and forth. Anxiety threatened to overwhelm me, but I was determined to stay calm to get to the bottom of this.

My mother pulled up, and before I could open the passenger door, she started yelling.

"What is going on, Tabitha? It's always something with you and this boy!" she exclaimed.

"Mom, I tried to tell you that Korey G. is dangerous, but you wouldn't listen to me! He pulled a gun on Montel this evening.

"What?!" she yelled.

"How does he have possession of a gun?" my mother questioned.

"Mom, I don't know! Can you please drive to the house so we can find out why Barak brought him up here?" I yelled.

My mother pulled off screeching tires. I sobbed the whole way home. I wanted answers from my brother, and he was going to give them to me.

Barak's car was backed up into the driveway. I had hopped out of the van while it was still moving, I discovered Barak and Korey G. sitting on the steps, chopping it up.

"What did you do? Why did you pull a gun on Montel?" I yelled.

They looked at me and were maddeningly calm.

"Barak! Why did you bring him up there?" I asked.

"I didn't know he had a gun on him. He told me that you were in trouble at school, and someone was attempting to jump on you, so I told him he could ride with me to get you." Barak shrugged.

"He lied to you!" I cried. "Why?" I asked, imploring Korey G. "Do you have any idea how livid people are going to be with me? He is a star football player! People already don't like me at school!"

My mother walked and stood behind me, her arms folded on her chest.

"You two thug, dropouts think you can just make my life harder at school. I am the one that has to deal with all the dirty looks and backlash," I explained.

"He shouldn't have been courting my girlfriend," Korey G. smirked.

"Girlfriend? I'm not your girlfriend! Tiara is your girlfriend! You think you can have your cake and eat it too? It doesn't work that way! When was the last time I spoke to you?"

Silence.

My mother stepped forward and started in. "Korey G., what did you do? Tabitha has a point. You guys haven't even been speaking, so she assumed you broke up. Now I'm hearing you pulled a gun out on the young man that Tabitha's dating?"

"I didn't pull a gun out on him; I just showed it to him," Korey G. replied.

"Why? Then you coax my son into taking you to the school? He could be an accessory if someone calls the cops," my mother explained.

Barak was getting concerned. "I don't have anything to do with this. Korey G. will go down for this alone. I didn't even know he had the gun. Hell, he lied to me."

"I did lie to him. I felt like I was losing my girl," Korey G. said.

"Korey G., I have watched you ride past my house every day for the last few weeks going to that girl's house that stay around the corner from us. So what is it that you want from my daughter? Leave her alone! I don't want my daughter in drama! If someone attempts to put their hands on her, they're going to have some major problems!" My mother's tone was a high-pitched threat.

I was over Korey G. and his shenanigans, and I just wanted him to leave me alone. Barak betrayed me for even bringing him up to school. I was finally making friends and gaining some sort of notoriety, and then this happened. People genuinely loved Montel, and I knew this was going to cause problems with him and me. I locked my bedroom door and stared up at the ceiling. Why was nothing going right for me? I couldn't catch a break.

Korey G. was so selfish and didn't have any reverence for anyone, not even my family. Was someone calling the cops right now and telling them Barak was the getaway driver? What did Korey G. say to Montel at gunpoint? I needed to talk to Montel.

There was a knock at my door, but I didn't answer.

"Tabitha, can I please talk to you? I told your mother I would apologize to you," Korey G. asked.

What? The audacity of this fool wanting to apologize to me for pulling a gun on my current boyfriend.

"I love you, man. I'm so sorry. I let my emotions get the best of me. I'm begging you to please forgive me. Give me a second chance!" he exclaimed.

As tough I wanted to be, he was breaking me down mentally, and he knew it. I slowly opened the door just enough to see his forehead.

"I'm listening," I said.

"Damn, Tabitha. I fucked up. The thing with Tiara, how I've treated you, pulling the gun on that boy at school... but I'm so in love with you. I cannot see you with anyone else," he cried.

Korey G.'s fighting words pulled at my heart. And suddenly, everything made sense. All of this turmoil was about me. I was Korey G's void the same way my bio dad was mine. That's why my life was nothing but chaos since we broke up. It was all so clear. I was pushing away a man who was fighting so hard for me. Not to mention how I felt when Montel pushed me aside after the game.

I opened my bedroom door and let him in.

Korey G.'s hug took my breath away.

He really does love me.

I assured Korey G. it was over, and we could work on restoring what we had.

I mean, who threatens someone with a gun? Someone who can't live without you.

If they really love you, they'll fight for you.

Chapter 11: Mayweather

My parents and I were fighting more, and I was rebelling to the hundredth power. Hopping out of windows, staying out late, getting in trouble at school, it was a never-ending cycle of Tabitha on the loose. I was feeling restless. I knew the world was bigger than this small town. My curiosity was taking over, and I wanted to know more beyond the routine of this little place on earth and its even smaller men.

I was tired of the lies Korey G. was telling me. My biological father loved glass dicks more than he did his family. My uncle was also in the streets. My step father was mentally checked out and not available. My brothers dropped out of school for no real reason. I was a girl amongst male failures with a mother trying to keep us afloat. And she was exhausting herself, putting out the fires that all these men created. I didn't want that for myself. *So why not be like the men?*

On this day in school, I arrived an hour late in the middle of a fire drill. One of the counselors hurried me into the overcrowded and chaotic auditorium to ensure the entire school followed procedure. We were released back into our regular classrooms five minutes later. I got a glass, bottled coke from the vending machine, took a sip, and walked into three husky Caucasian females blocking the way.

I said, "Can I help you?"

They were quiet at first until one of them said, "You stepped on my friend's toe during the fire drill, and you need to apologize!"

I busted out laughing and said, "We are no longer in slavery, and I don't have to apologize for something that was clearly unintentional." I pushed my way through the three of them. After a few steps, a bottle crashed against my eye, and I staggered back. When I gained my balance, I grabbed the closest one around the neck and started punching her in the face. I fell to the ground with my arm still gripped tightly around her neck. The crowd cheered loudly as the fight ensued. Suddenly, I was lifted to my feet from behind, so I pivoted and started swinging until I realized it was one of my old teammates.

"Run, run!" she cried.

I took off, running in the opposite direction of the office. Blind authority always reinforced its own power. What did it matter if I was in the right or wrong? What mattered was that they maintained an example of their authority. I respected my mother but realized she was powerless over my brothers because they didn't hold themselves in high esteem. And continuously trying to live right while others are living wrong is not only a lonely place to be, but drains your soul.

I ran to the nearest bathroom. Of all places, my refuge was a nasty school bathroom with its sharp smell of cheap soap and piss-stained walls. At least it was empty. I locked the stall door behind me and knelt by the toilet to examine myself. My adrenaline continued to pump, as blood dripped from my right hand and knuckles. I struggled to catch my breath.

I didn't plan on being whacked in the face with a bottle, but that is life. *Do I fight or get beaten down?* I was too feisty to stay down, but how do I stay standing?

I knew I was in so much trouble. I heard heavy steps approaching, and I braced myself. Should I have just stood my ground and owned the situation out there in front of all those kids?

I heard a voice of authority calling my name.

"Tabitha. Are you in here?"

I opened the stall. I shivered, and my skin was sticky with blood. I felt like a wounded bird, whose wings were clipped by circumstance, but maybe I looked like a perpetrator to them.

"You need to come with me," Principal Skinner convinced me.

Principal Skinner escorted me to the office, where we passed by the three white girls sitting in the lobby waiting to be informants. Their grins meant their privileged white girl voices would muffle mine. Clearly, I was outnumbered, but was I outclassed as well? I had always heard of racism in the community, but because I played sports and was a star athlete, I never experienced it. I wondered if they would just walk away with nothing but a warning.

Principal Skinner told me to have a seat as she phoned my mother at work. She obviously did not care for my side of the story and made the assumption that I was the aggressor. I didn't fear anybody but Mom Dukes and disappointing her was worse than death. I believed I saw my heart pounding through my chest.

"Mrs. Edwards, I am afraid your daughter has been in an altercation at school, and because of it, she'll be expelled for the next five days."

The world was created in seven days, and my demise would take five.

"We are going to need someone to come pick her up," the principal said and tapped her pencil on her desk calendar. That may have been just another workday for her, but didn't she realize my life was in her hands? Who were all these people now deciding who I was and what I was about?

As Principal Skinner matter-of-factly related to my mother the details of the pending suspension, I watched as the three girls conversed with the counselor and pointed in my direction. *Wait a second.* The counselor looked concerned and glanced over at me with disgust as she shook her large head from side-to-side. A fury instantly surged and propelled me out of the principal's office, over the counter, and plowed my fist into the nearest girl's face. This was what rage felt like, and I relished in it. Two more glorious punches later, I was snatched up by the counselor and a football player.

Three white girls started up with me, one unsuspecting black girl. I didn't kiss their feet, so they struck me like a mule. This was racial, and this was common, but it was my turn now, my coming-of-age passage, to endure being struck and dehumanized only to be punished for defending my humanity. My pride prevented me from going out like a sucker, and I wonder if those girls remembered the feeling of my fist. I was only a freshman, but already *the nobody* in high school. I wanted to earn my respect, and I wanted them all to feel my wrath.

They dragged me back into the office to sit with the principal, and this time they closed the door to make sure the sight of the door being closed would somehow restrain me.

"What happened?" my mother screamed at me as I got on the phone.

I told her the whole story, making sure the principal heard me.

"Three white girls..." I began as I looked into my principal's eyes. She shifted in her seat and pulled at her skirt as if suddenly conscious of her pale legs.

"All I tried to do was to walk past them, but they said I'd stepped on one of their toes during the fire drill, and they wanted me to pay for that." I continued, as I glared at the principal. "Then, when I tried to go around, they cracked me upside the head with a bottle." The principal looked up.

"What was I going to do, Mama? Let them beat me up like that because I am the new black girl at school? Why do I have to go here anyways, Mama? Is that what school is all about? Beat the black kids down, so they leave?"

By now, the principal looked at me impatiently.

No, you're going to listen to this, I thought to myself. *I may not ever sit on the other side of a desk like this, but I am at this desk now.*

While I tormented the principal with the reality of the situation, my actions were not appropriate. Maybe if I'd cried and taken the beating; I would have been sitting out there and not in here. I was no animal, but I was too proud. I hoped my mother would realize that there was no other way than the one I'd chosen.

After a long period of silence, she said, "Did you let them feel it, baby girl?"

"Yes, ma'am," I responded proudly.

"Good, because I never raised a coward. I'm on my way to get you!" she exclaimed.

I smirked at the principal as I handed her the phone. My mom *always* has my back.

Chapter 12: On the Prowl

As we drove away from the high school, my mother casually explained how justice works when you're a black girl. My verdict: suspended for five days. The white girls' verdict: The white girls who targeted me for their day's delight—two days apiece. My mother was kind of upset. My mother was not naïve to this breed of inequality, but she taught us that fairness ruled the day.

After that episode, my mother wanted to get me away from harsh reality to a more convenient, sheltered existence. The next morning, we drove in her 1995 bronze Volkswagen Jetta (a car my mother couldn't seem to part ways with) to the local high school in Oxford, North Carolina . Now Oxford also was an exceedingly small hick town. But the environment seemed a little bit more diverse. The local girls who were attending school there used to come to the pizza parlor that my step dad managed, and they seemed nice. I never bonded with females over primping and looking pretty. They didn't like basketball as I did, so I didn't share much in common with them. As we got closer to the school, I felt a sense of relief.

As we walked into the lobby of this newfangled environment, it seemingly brought some peace. It resembled my current high school in terms of the layout, but I was inhaling fresh paint on the cement walls.

We headed towards the front office so my mother could explain the situation and petition for me to attend this school after my suspension was completed. They declined my enrollment because I didn't live within the school district. I have my bio father's con artist gene, so if it were up to me, I would have used somebody else's address. But my mother was a saint, and would not do anything crooked. However, she wasn't pleased with their response, and she planned to escalate her request to the next level, but we'd deal with this situation tomorrow.

We pulled up in front of our house, and I jumped out of the car, assuming she had to return to work. I watched from the living room window as she pulled away. I wondered what the next several days had in store for me. My mother was overly ambitious but didn't want to get my hopes up about the new school.

I slept in the following morning as my mother set off on her mission in solitude. She went to the superintendent's office and pled her case. But they still declined my enrollment due to the severity of the fight. The decision makers taking control of the narrative flipped the script to fit into their reality, where I was the crazed aggressor who bullied three older girls. It made no sense to me, but this new school bought it. I was stuck. Now I had two options: Go back to school and face these liars or I could just be a high school dropout.

Both of my mother's sons were high school dropouts, and I didn't think she could endure that heartbreak again. She placed her chips of hope on me. Besides dropping out because of three bullies would paint me a coward, something not tolerated in my mother's home. She always wondered where she went wrong with my brothers, and felt she had raised me to be tough and to endure. And that made sense because my father wasn't around, my brothers were doing their own thing, and my step father was busy working. My mother was very hard on herself as a parent, and I know she wondered how I negotiated my place in the world.

I finally asked my step dad for a part-time job to occupy my time, not knowing I would really like working. I was good at it too. I started off waitressing first, but then I went to take orders via phone, to running the cash register, then to opening the store on the weekends. I was making good cash for a teenager, and that was a little bit addictive. I was going home pocketing $80 to $100 a day, and it felt good to earn my own. I met a lot of friendly faces, and I was able to make friends while working there. I was thinking, *I could really make this my thing!*

The next week rolled around, and it was time for school. I woke up feeling sluggish and did everything I possibly could to pass the time. My mother yelled at me from the top of her lungs, but I didn't care. I was still having issues with my boyfriend, so school was way down on my list of priorities. School was a waste of eight hours when I was supposed to be getting to the money. I needed a car, and that wasn't going to happen by me sitting around them teachers all day. My mother dropped me off at the front door, and I watched as she drove away. I stood in front of the breezeway for ten minutes, and then I walked in. School had already started, so I signed in late and headed to first period.

When I walked into class, it was awkward. It was almost as if I was a celebrity, or possibly even popular now due to that brawl last week. As soon as I sat down, people started passing notes, asking me if we were going to fight again. Then they talked about my opponent's eye and a whole bunch of other crap I'd no desire to hear. I balled the notes up, slumped down in my seat, and doodled in my notebook the remainder of the class. What happened at lunchtime was very telling for me. People walked up to me, giving me dap and high fives. That's when I realized; this isn't the place I want to be. People glorify raucous fights and innocent people getting hurt. I knew right then that I was attending my last day of school. Besides, I was working and planned on getting a place with Korey G., and we were going to live happily ever after.

The next morning rolled around, and I didn't respond to my mother yelling at me at all. She busted in the room, snatched the covers off me, and demanded I got dressed for school. I sat up on the side of the bed, looked at her with a straight face, and said, "I'm not going back to that school ever again!"

"What do you mean? Who are you talking to like that?" she exclaimed.

"I'm going to work and save up for Korey G. and me to get a place!" I said.

My mother stared at me for a minute, and I knew I was about to get my butt kicked all over that house. After the long pause, she turned and walked out. I sat and waited for her to return with a belt. Instead, awhile later, I heard the front door slam. A part of me wanted her to put up a fight, and a part of me didn't. I always think if she would have just argued with me that morning about getting dressed, maybe I wouldn't have been a high school dropout.

My parents were also looking to buy a house more rooted in the countryside. I knew they had plans to do so, but I wasn't aware when that was going to happen. There was complete silence at the dinner table that night until my step father announced that they closed on a house and we were relocating about fifteen minutes from our current home. I started throwing things and yelling at the top of my lungs about how unfair it was. All I could think about was being an additional fifteen to twenty minutes from Korey G. I guess my oldest brother was sick and tired of hearing about him, so he blurted out, "Why are you so into that dude? He isn't thinking about you! Plus, he got a baby on the way by Tiara!" he said.

My heart dropped, but I stood my ground! My brothers were remarkably familiar with Tiara because she had tried to push up on both of them at one point. Even though what they said was possible, I refused to believe it.

"Liar! You're a liar! I hate you! None of you want me to be happy! I hate all of you!" I roared as I ran out of the house. I grabbed my basketball and sprinted for the woods. My adrenaline was pumping so hard; I felt as if I were about to pass out. As I approached the woods, I fell to my knees and cried out to God.

"Why are you letting this happen to me?" I pleaded with Him.

I spent the next forty minutes, yelling obscenities at God, but He never responded.

A few minutes later, someone was yelling my name. I didn't respond at all. Shortly after, someone lifted me off the ground, and if it were a rapist or murderer that would have been fine with me because I just wanted to die. However, it was my older brother picking me up off the ground and holding me in his arms. He was silent, which meant he was hurting for me. He sobbed too because older brothers didn't want to see their sister get hurt. He grabbed my hand, but I couldn't move. He picked me up in his arms like a baby and walked me a mile back to the house. He put me in the passenger side of his red Honda civic. It felt as though he was driving for hours before he spoke.

"Tabitha, I am so sorry. I cannot believe I let this happen. This is all my fault. I was supposed to protect you," he said.

I instantly stopped weeping because anybody that knew Saul, knew he was quiet. He never expressed himself at all, and he stayed by his lonesome. He told me how I deserved better and how that wasn't what love looked like. *How in the hell did he know about love?* Saul gave up on the one girl that loved and cared for him because she was a virgin. She was waiting on her husband before she got between the sheets with anybody. He was so sincere and made valid points. **But that still didn't take the pain away.**

The next day, I was determined to move on, but I needed answers. Korey G. was not picking up the phone. I got dressed and ready for work. I was too young to be going through this. The average fifteen-year-old didn't go through this type of stuff. My other friends were normal, but then again, I no longer had those friends because I was a high school dropout. It hurt. It hurt so badly. This was the perfect time for this so-called God my mother always talked about to show up.

My mother's step father turned up at our house early Saturday morning because it was time for us to move into our new home. Saul and I weren't receptive to the move at all. Besides, they were moving us an additional fifteen to twenty minutes from what was considered the city. We helped load the truck and waved goodbye to our parents. We informed them we would meet them out there, but we never showed up. Saul and I were determined to stay behind and consider that our own place. This idea was insane because we had no furniture, no food, and no telephone. All we had was his little red car, a few blankets, and each other. I cannot tell you what was going through our brains as our parents and the knee baby got settled into our new house, and we stayed behind.

My step father saw my oldest brother and me at work, and we ignored his questions about why we had not come to the new house yet. It was only a matter of time before the new owners would start surfacing and looking to rent the place. However, we were determined to wait it out.

It had been weeks since I heard from Korey G., which wasn't normal. I was sitting in the front yard one day, and I heard his car. Korey G. had the loudest system in the city, and you could hear him coming a mile away. As he passed by me, the passenger seat was occupied by the alleged baby mother. I was determined to wait him out, and if he refused to stop and talk to me, I would just jump in front of his car. Four hours passed by, and just as I was about to give up and go in the house, I heard his car coming over the speed bump. To my surprise, he slowed down, cut his car off, and sat with his head hanging down in silence.

"Is it true?" I asked.

There was dead silence, which indicated it was true that he was expecting a baby.

"Answer me!" I exclaimed.

"What do you want me to say? I messed up!" he yelled as tears start streaming down his face.

"My life is over! She trapped me!" he pleaded.

"*Trapped* you, Korey G.? *How does a woman trap you?*" I asked through my own tears.

It wasn't rocket science that if you have unprotected sex, you're asking to get pregnant. I pondered the whole "*trapped*" comment but I was still vulnerable, and suddenly, I was cradling his head and holding him as we wept together.

This was all my fault!

"I'm ready now," I whispered. Korey G. stopped crying.

"Are you serious? Are you sure? Why now?" he asked. I placed my finger on his lips and motioned for him to come to the empty house with me. We'd previously attempted to have sex a couple of dozen times, but it hurt so badly that I made him stop. He closed my bedroom door and stared at me like I was his last meal. I fixed the blankets on the floor and slowly started dropping my basketball shorts. I didn't feel sexy at all, but I'd like to win him back. Of course, this wouldn't change the fact that he was having a kid, but *I* would be his girl. I was happy with that. He laid me down on the pallet that I'd been sleeping on for days.

Korey G. started kissing me all over my body. I mean everywhere. I felt weird in a good way. I had never heard of foreplay. That went on for twenty minutes, and I could not stop moaning and shaking. After that, he proceeded with penetration.

That was the most uncomfortable and painful feeling I'd ever felt in my life. I squirmed and slid until my head hit the wall. We'd been through this before, and I didn't follow through, but this time had to be different. I closed my eyes and braced myself. He started stroking up and down, and the more he moaned, the more tears ran down the side of my face. I was so confused at this point because the girls on the basketball team told me this sex thing felt good. All I did was pray to God that this would be over quick.

When it was over, I sat in the corner with my basketball shorts balled up in my hand and blood in my vaginal area. Nobody told me that having sex would make your period come on. This was so gross!

He came close to me and said, "What's wrong?"

"Is this supposed to be love? *Is love supposed to hurt?*"

I broke down crying, and all I felt was the warmth of his body and his arms wrapped around me. Now *that* was, by far, the best feeling ever. I guess guys needed to *feel* you to know that they are loved. We sat like this for hours, wrapped up in each other until I finally fell asleep.

The next morning there was a knock at the door. It was the landlord informing us that he was about to bring in cleaners, and he was under the impression that the premises were vacated. I assured him that my brother and I just had a few more things to gather, and we'd be out in a few hours. I went and woke up Saul. At that point, we had no option but to go to the new house.

When we pulled up the driveway of our new house, my mother opened the front door and said, "You two finally came to your senses, I see."

Saul and I trudged past her in silence. I entered my new room and flopped on my bed. I missed Korey G., I didn't want to stay in the country, and my life was literally at a standstill. I went from being a virgin athlete with a bright future to giving myself to someone who was a high school dropout with a baby on the way with another woman. Life was just about to get a little worse.

Because we lived so far out, I needed to get my license. However, my mother told me that until she saw some improvement in my decision-making, she wasn't carrying me under her insurance. To top that off, she sat me down and told me Korey G. wasn't welcomed at our new home due to recent events with at the park and the gun incident on school grounds. I didn't get it. My mother never really had those birds and the bee's talks with me, so I wondered if she was oblivious to the fact that I might be sexually active, or she just didn't care to know. I called Korey G. and told him the news, and he started yelling on the phone.

"How are we going to be together? You have to make a decision. Your family, or me? Or else this is over!" he said and promptly hung up.

A few months later, Korey G. and I plotted that I would stay with him at his sister's house. So, after my parents fell asleep one night, I hopped out the side window attached to my bedroom and waited at the end of the dark street for him to show up. And sure enough, five minutes later, he pulled up, and I hopped in. I was so happy! We were finally going to be together with no worries. All I wanted was to work and come home to him. His sister's trailer park wasn't in the best neighborhood. When we got to her house, I noticed the carpet was filthy. I wasn't used to living like that, but I wanted to be wherever Korey G. was. I put my stuff down on his bed and walked to the bathroom. I flipped on the light, and roaches scattered everywhere. I ran out of the bathroom.

"Did you find the bathroom okay?" he asked.

"Yes, but there are bugs in there!" I replied.

"Oh, so you're too good to stay where a few bugs are? If you feel that way, I can take your ass back to your mother's house, so you can be miserable. But don't call me complaining that you miss me," he said.

I assured him that I was perfectly okay with the living conditions, and I kissed his forehead.

Korey G. was driving me to and from work, and things seemed fine until he said that I had to give him my whole paycheck because we had to pay bills. Bills? I was still a kid! I guess these are

279

the sacrifices you make if you want to live on your own and act grown.

After a week, I started wondering why my mother hadn't tried to find me. Until one day, Korey G. answered a knock at the door. He looked out the peephole, and the way he turned to look at me with an impatient demeanor, I knew it was my mother. It felt as though I was being swallowed up by quicksand, as Korey G. opened the door, stepped outside, and closed it softly behind him.

My head slumped between my legs, and I shook uncontrollably. When the shouting started, I jumped to my feet and started pacing.

What was I going to do?

I knew that opening that door would infuriate Korey G. But this altercation was all my fault, and that was my mother.

I threw the door open and said, "That's enough!"

My mother looked fatigued, her eyes were wild as she stood with her hands on her hips. "I'm glad you finally came out! Get your things; you're going home with us!"

My non-confrontational step dad looked sheepish, standing off to the side. I explained that this was my new home now, and I wasn't budging.

"I cannot believe you, Tabitha! We have a brand-new home, and you want to stay over here in this roach-infested trailer park!" my mother said.

"That's your problem. You're so judgmental, and you don't want me to be happy!" I cried.

"Tabitha, you're fifteen years old and a high school dropout. What do you know about being happy over here, shacking up with this grown man? You know what? Don't even worry about it!" she said.

And then she disappeared in-between two trailers.

What was she going to do now?

Korey G. and I retreated into the house.

He said, "Maybe you should just pack your things and go with your mom."

"What do you mean? You don't love me anymore? Why are you acting this way?"

"Man, your mother is probably going to call the cops, and I don't have time for that type of drama over here. I refuse to go to jail for some underage pussy! Just go!" he yelled.

Was that all I was to him?

"No! I will not go! I live here too, and I will not be forced out by her!" I replied.

During this heated argument, there was a loud knock at the door.

"Butner Police! Open up!"

I opened the door, and an officer said, "Are you, Tabitha? If so, you need to come with us."

I was devastated. I looked over at my mother's gloating face. I tried to shut the door, but it bounced back off the officer's foot. As I walked into the room to grab my things, all I could think about was all of this fuss resembled a drug raid. Really? All of this for me. I wasn't impressed at all. Korey G. wouldn't even make eye contact as I left. I guess it was over for us. My tears blinded me to all the involved parties. As I got closer to the MVP van, my mother grabbed my arm, and I jerked it away from her and collapsed into the back seat where I wept uncontrollably. My step dad just stood there in silence with this frustrated look on his face as he always did.

But then I noticed my mother engaging in a serious conversation with the cops who were about to handcuff Korey G. I jumped out of the van and ran over to him screaming,

"No! No! No! What are you guys doing? All he is guilty of is loving me! Please don't do this!" I yelled.

I begged my mother with every fiber of my being to not have him arrested. I was fully aware that Korey G. was technically engaged in statutory rape because he was eighteen, and I was fifteen.

"Take the handcuffs off. *This time*," my mother said.

"*"Stay away from my daughter!"* she yelled before closing the driver's side door.

I got back into the van and we drove away in complete silence. Now exiting the trailer park involved lots of twists and turns. The last stretch was a long hill that came to a stop sign. As the van approached the stop sign, I opened the door and jumped out of the van while it was moving. I rolled into a fence and came to a stop.

My mother screamed after me. I jumped up, dusted myself off, and began to run blindly back to the trailer park at full speed. I had no idea where I was going, but I knew I didn't want to go with my parents.

I got midway up the hill when my mother's van passed me at full speed. I stopped in my tracks. She was racing back to inform the police that I'd escaped her care and that I was combative. I'd be placed in custody.

I knew how this looked. This was all over a guy that was going to move on and be with the next female the moment he knew that my availability had been severed. And then the swiftly-approaching sirens, being handcuffed, and put in the back of the car.

I was a complete failure, just like my bio dad. As we arrived at the precinct, they escorted me inside and sat me on a bench. I was so mentally and physically exhausted that I didn't ask any questions. Some guy who looked like a supervisor started questioning me, but I remained silent.

How did I end up here?

"Young lady, if you don't start talking, we're going to have to dress you out and put you in the cell with some very bad people. Now is that what you want?" the officer asked.

"Sir, no offense to you, but I just want to go home. Back to my boyfriend's house," I responded.

He explained to me how my so-called boyfriend was breaking the law by allowing me to stay there and that a nice girl like me needed to be with her parents.

I looked up at him and asked him if he would find my father.

He said, "Your father is at home with your mother waiting on you!"

"That's not my father. My father's name is Don Royster. Could you find him for me, please? I would like to go to his house instead of going home with my mother and her husband. I'm old enough now, and I have that option. Please. Just look him up."

The officer agreed and walked off.

After a while, he returned with paperwork and took a seat close to me.

"Young lady, is there something going on at home that you care to disclose to me? Otherwise, I think you returning there may be the safest place for you at this time", he said.

Then he proceeded to hand me the paperwork: My father's mugshot plastered ten pages of arrest records displaying all sorts of charges along with his current incarceration. I shoved the paperwork back at the officer and requested to go home to my mother. It was crystal-clear that I had nowhere to go. I was embarrassed more than anything, and I didn't want to hear her lip and to get drenched in holy oil. I was clearly the devil right about now.

My mother arrived an hour later to take me home. Neither of us had anything to say. What do you say to somebody who's ruining your life? It never dawned on me that she was attempting to protect me or that I was selfish and self-absorbed at the time. But as we pulled in the driveway, I looked up at the beautiful home that my parents had purchased and realized I was being a brat. I opened the van door and got out. I walked through the house, and my brothers were sitting in the living room, staring at me as if I was some type of weirdo. I grabbed a paper cup from the kitchen and headed straight for my room.

The next couple of days were hard for me. My mother had taken my phone away. My mother would answer the house phone and repeatedly say I was grounded or to stop calling me. One of those callers had to be him. I locked myself in my room for the next four days, refusing to come out for food, water, or the bathroom. I just peed in that cup and poured it out the window. I cried out all my tears. If only someone had schooled me on soul ties and how they kept you emotionally bonded to someone, then maybe I would have been more prepared when this separation anxiety surfaces.

On day four, my step dad knocked on my door, asking me to come out. I hesitated for a second but felt excited that someone was coming to see about me. I came out wearing the same clothes that I'd returned home in. As I walked into the living room, my mother's face turned red, and she teared up. Sheesh, did I look that bad? My step dad said that he was totally against everything that I was putting my mother through. However, if it made me happy to be back over there with that boy, he supported my decision to go back. I instantly got happy and ran over to hug him, but he stopped me with his hand. I don't know if that was because I'd not showered in four days or because this was a part of the tough-love process. I slowly backed up and looked up at my mother. She was crying her eyes out.

"Ma?" I said.

"Leave me alone, Tabitha!" she said and stormed out of the room.

I was hurting everybody, but I didn't care. All I cared about was myself and getting back over there to that man.

I called Korey G. and gave him the good news. He was hesitant at first; however, he hung up and appeared at the end of my driveway. I tried to go in and have a few words with my mother, but she refused to talk to me. My bags hadn't moved from the front porch in four days because *nobody was bringing any bugs into her house.*

I kissed Korey G., he smiled, and we rode off into the sunset. *Just kidding.*

My reunion with Korey G. was a disaster. The baby mama kept popping up at all hours of the night, upset because we were back together. I had to contain my anger and try not to fight her because they had a child together. Korey G. started hitting me in the back of the head, calling me stupid and taking my money. And when things were really good, I could look forward to lying like a possum when he had an erection. My stubborn pride dictated that going home meant they won, they were right, and that I would lose my man.

That pride would be the death of me.

Weeks went by, and I woke up unhappier and unhealthier by the day. When my brother picked me up for work, he scolded me about dropping so much weight. Korey G. was pressuring me about bringing more money in even though I was already working two jobs: One at the pizza parlor and the other working at my grandmother's cafe. Hell, my grandmother was only paying my brother and me $100 a week. Is this what high school dropouts made? The financial stress killed my appetite.

My brother and I conjured up a plan to make a little money on the side. I would put aside every big bill that came through the register. My brother would scoop them up when he made deposits, pocketed them, and we would profit fifty/fifty. Was it right? Nope. But we needed the money.

I waited on this Caucasian guy who frequented the café, and he would give me marijuana for free. He probably assumed I was older because I was curvy for my age. This wasn't your average marijuana. So, I was pocketing that too and taking it home for Korey G. to sell. I never saw that pay off.

My grandmother's café brought in other older male customers who showered me with gifts and extra funds based solely on the way I looked. I couldn't believe they thought I was pretty and how easily they let go of their money. The men would slide me their business cards when my grandmother wasn't looking and whisper for me to call them.

I did not recognize all the ways that Korey G. was using me. I was stealing from my own grandmother, passing along drugs, and working my ass off—all of this for a man who was making me feel less than.

When my mind got quiet, I wanted to just lay in my mother's lap, have her run her hand through my hair, and assure me everything was going to be okay.

I was becoming a terrible person.

That was my life for two months until my grandmother figured out that my brother and I had been stealing. She never said one word. She just didn't allow my brother and me to operate the register anymore. So, my well ran dry quickly, as it should have because we were dead wrong to steal in the first place. Once I wasn't bringing in money like that to the house anymore, Korey G.'s attitude hit new lows, and so did my tolerance.

One early Saturday morning, I acted like I was leaving for work, hid in the woods, and once I saw Korey G. was gone, I doubled-backed, packed all my things, and didn't look back.

When I arrived at my mother's house, the smell of bacon and eggs wafted through the screen door. It felt so refreshing to be back home, but I wasn't sure if my mother was going to be receptive or not. I stood in the driveway, suddenly realizing my own mother might reject me. I heard the latch unlock and saw this pretty redbone standing at the door.

"Come on," my mother said as if she'd been expecting me all along.

I dropped my things and ran to the door. I reached out in an attempt to give her the biggest hug this side of the Mississippi, but she stopped me dead in my tracks.

"Oh no! I don't know where you been! Leave them clothes and that mess right here at this front porch. Strip! Right now, before you come in my house! You look like something off the Buzzer Root!" she yelled.

Nobody knew what the Buzzer Root was, but my mother used this frequently when referring to someone who looked a mess.

"Oh Mama! It's me!" I said.

"Now come on in here and get cleaned up. I got you a hot breakfast waiting on you. I knew you was coming back," she said, trying to fight back tears.

My mother was the goat when it came to displaying grace. I walked through our brand-new home, nude, and straight to the bathroom that I shared with my brothers. I jumped in the clean snow-white shower and twirled around a few times until I was startled by a knock at the door. It was my mother bringing me fresh linen. I was super relieved to be in a clean home and in my mother's presence. There was something so soothing about being with family.

I must have stayed in the shower for forty minutes until I heard her calling my name, telling me that my breakfast was going to get cold. We stayed in the country parts now and that well water didn't get cold, so I could have stayed in there all day. As I jumped out of the shower and toweled myself off, I caught a glimpse of myself in the mirror and noticed the spread in my hip area. My breasts were growing and rounding out as well. I wondered if these new accentuating features were attributed to having sex.

I laid across my bed and sunk into the expensive mattress my parents had purchased me. It hit me hard how ungrateful and unappreciative I was. I had just been there a few days before but hadn't noticed the stuffed animals and all of the other nice girly things my mother had lovingly planted in my room. I had some apologizing to do.

Things were awkward at first. However, after some time, we were all able to reconcile our relationships. My grandmother fired me after she told my mother about my brother and me stealing from her. I started working at the pizza parlor full-time, which was more structured and had cameras, so I had to walk a straight line. The money was more than decent when the local dope boys came in on Friday and Saturday nights. The Pizza Parlor was the hotspot in Oxford. I was exposed to a lot early in the game, and all the local drug dealers had a thing for *old Spaulding*.

My brothers also worked there, so we managed the restaurant for my dad. To set the atmosphere as if it was a nightclub, I lined up a playlist on the jukebox with nothing but Biggie and Aaliyah. Dancing and drinking emptied their pockets. I learned to hustle at an early age, and it was in my blood. But inside, I was short on confidence and felt like damaged goods after being with Korey G.

I got home from work one day to my step brother sitting in the living room with all his luggage in the corner. Keaton, Jr. visited us occasionally, and he was close to my brothers. However, he had never bought this much luggage before. It was cool having him around at times because he was more attentive to me than my brothers. Besides, Keaton, Jr. was the only child that actually visited our home. I didn't know if my step dad even spoke to his daughter throughout the years. I would have liked to have a sister, but that seemed unlikely.

My step brother and I were the same age, but he went to a different school in Durham because he still lived with his mother. My understanding was that he was a problem child.

I found my mother in her retreat area and whispered, "What is he doing here?"

My mother let out a big sigh and said, "He's going to be living with us for a while. His mother is fed up with his behavior, and she sent him to live with us."

"Huh? We don't have any room for him, and we don't need that drama," I said.

"Shh-hhh, lower your voice. He can hear you," she said.

"I don't care, mom; he can't stay here. It was bad enough the boys and I were already fighting for the shower in the mornings. Now, I have to deal with another dirty boy. Great!" I said.

As the weeks passed, we started hanging out in my room, watching TV, chatting, or playing video games. My brothers made fun of him because he was always hanging around a "girl." Little did they know, this kid had a motive.

One night my parents were out, leaving me with my oldest brother and step brother. I was in a deep sleep when I woke to my step brother standing over me with his hands down my pants.

"What are you doing?" I yelled.

He placed his hand over my mouth and told me to be quiet.

"If you even attempt to mention this, your parents will just send you away. I heard them talking about it the other night. I know about you running away and being a hoe already. No one will believe you," he said.

It was true. I felt so betrayed by my parents. Why were they telling this thug my business? I just laid there as he touched my breasts and played in my vagina. I was so numb at this point; it didn't matter. He would literally cum in me and then whisper an antagonizing reminder that I would be evicted from the home of the only parents I knew.

That was my worth to the opposite sex.

This scenario went on for months. Each incident sent me reeling to the bathroom where I vomited. It was only by the grace of God that I didn't get pregnant.

During that time, I was standoffish with my entire family. Even conversations with my mother ended abruptly. I was so tired of him humping on me, but if I disclosed to my mother what he was doing, the chaos and opposition would possibly end her marriage. I had already caused so many problems in the household and I certainly wasn't credible, so I kept the *secret*. We were *not* going back to that hood that my brothers talked about. It was time for me to circumvent a different route, to stop being subjected to his demons.

At this point, I started to pick up extra hours at the pizza parlor so I could avoid all contact at the house with Keaton Jr.

One customer at work caught my eye. Ken came around on weekends. He drove a flashy car, dressed nice, and wore tons of jewelry. Ken was tall and had the most beautiful brown eyes I'd ever seen in my life. When he asked me out, I was on top of the world. He was the hottest local drug dealer around. He bought me nice things, gave me money, and even let me drive his car. Ken was really into me, especially since I could drive a five-speed. But boy, was I in for a rude awakening! This man had baby-mama drama and she would come to my job looking for "her baby-daddy." The way these women acted over a man was some powerful birth control for me.

Around this time, my step father purchased a white neon for me, but I wasn't happy with it. I wanted something foreign to drive like the other kids I had noticed a school. *Ma always said comparison was the thief of joy.* I complained about it daily, but Ken always wanted to trade cars. I drove his car to work, and he met me at his house when I got off work. My desires to be away from the house manifested expeditiously.

Little did I know that his Honda Accord was a stolen vehicle. I could have been in so much trouble, but once again, God assisted me in dodging another bullet. Our "relationship" consisted of going to the trap house after work and lying in the back room until Ken was horny. That got old quick, and on top of that, I learned the feds were watching him. I may have been entitled, naïve, and vulnerable, but I wasn't stupid. So that situation ended abruptly.

In the meantime, a tall, older man with the most beautiful brown eyes flashed on my radar. He also smelled incredibly fresh, dressed beautifully, and from our few conversations, seemed decent. I asked the assistant manager, who always had the tea, what his story was. I learned that he was a hustler too. I wanted him!

This man started patronizing the pizza shop four to five days a week. He'd wink at me before ordering his food. While flirting and bantering back and forth, one of my colleagues acted weird every time he came in. She would start to engage in random conversations with me and flaunt herself around the front area in hopes that he would notice her. One day, I discovered they had been sleeping together as recently as three weeks ago. Just then, he walked for another session of flirting and food.

"Are you having a good day, baby girl?" he smiled.

"I guess so," I responded with a feisty tone, noticing his crooked front teeth. But the more we interacted, the more I was intrigued. This time, he asked for my number, and I obliged.

Chapter 13: The Mama's Boy

His name was Wade, and the first thing I identified about him was that he was a mama's boy. He was intelligent, handsome, sexually-gifted, and his dope boy swag left me with no complaints. But I was in for a rude awakening. He lived with his divorced mother, so she was almost always at the house. But when she got a new man, that meant more freedom for us. Sex was amazing with Wade. I literally could not keep my hands off him. When his mother was at the house, we'd park and get it inside of the car or wherever we could to avoid having to sneak around her.

My family loved him, and things were going great. The only thing was, we couldn't do anything without this mother. If he wanted to take me out for seafood in Durham, a forty-five-minute drive, she'd tag along. That was new and confusing for me. Like I loved my mom and all, but I didn't want her with my man and myself every single time we had an outing. If we got into a disagreement, his mom noticed my absence and questioned him about my whereabouts. Then Wade would break down and tell her whatever it was that happened. Before you knew it, Ma was passing me the phone, saying Wade's mother wanted to speak to me.

She would always talk about how good of a man Wade was and how he meant well. That may have been true, but he simply wasn't listening to my concerns. One thing I despise is not being heard. It's an indication that you don't care about what I'm saying, because you don't care enough about me. If that was the case, I was ready to move on, but I'd miss his family. I always longed to date men with big families because my own family just didn't create that comfortable and fun vibe that you see in other families. We never had family reunions, family vacations, or family outings. But Wade just didn't want anything more for himself. He was content selling his pounds of marijuana, living in Oxford with his mother, and raving about her macaroni and cheese. I had the restless stirrings of escape, but my love and loyalty grounded me there.

A year later, we were still doing the same things over and over. I talked about us moving into our own place. Hell, I was nineteen years old and over Oxford. Oxford was a place where people got stuck. You graduate from high school, get a "good" job at the factory, get married, and start a family. I wanted to see the world and what else life had to offer.

Chapter 14: Motion of Discovery

Sadly, Ma's little brother, the one she used to get dressed before school in his younger days, the one that used to babysit us when my mom went out, became an addict. Uncle Nino was also in and out of jail throughout my life, and I didn't understand why. My grandmother enabled him by bailing him out every time he was incarcerated or cleaning up the latest mess he'd made.

When I was younger, my uncle was the closest thing to a dad because he helped Ma out a lot with us. I remember being mad at him because he was always locked up. He'd make promises to stay clean and out of prison, which fell on my young deaf ears due to his habitual behavior. The first time I visited him in prison, I vowed never to see him again. It hurt so much to see him chained up like an animal. But Ma wanted me to go along for a visit anyway.

As we arrived at the prison, I remember smelling this stench of dirty socks, stale sweat and urine that I knew was permeating my clothes, my hair, and my nose. We waited for the guard to bring my uncle out behind thick, smeared glass. I was mad that he put himself and us in this situation. But as soon as I heard his voice, I began to glow.

"Hey, Niece! Baby girl! How are you?" he said.

I was his only niece so that became a nickname he referenced as he addressed me when he called from prison.

I started to warm to him more, and he promised me for the fifth time, he wouldn't return to this awful place. I smiled. But a familiar wave of doubt arose. My uncle, who had once been like a father to me, was just another man in my life offering nothing but disappointment.

As we left the jail, I stared at the decrepit old building as Ma drove away until it was out of sight.

"Are you okay?" she asked.

"I'm okay, Ma. Do you think he's telling the truth this time about staying free and clean of those horrible drugs?" I asked.

Ma looked at me and smiled, "Yes, he will, baby girl."

307

When Ma told me something, I believed her. Her response gave me so much peace.

Shy of sixty days, my uncle was released. By this time, I was approaching another trip around the sun, becoming twenty years old and seeking something new. It seemed as if I was never content in my early adulthood; I was looking for that next adrenaline rush. I'd visit my uncle often in Durham just to check up on his progress. He got back on his feet, and I noticed some way and somehow, he was getting to the money. All of a sudden, my uncle was buying expensive cars, jewelry, clothes, and he had some of the *coldest* women I'd ever seen in that area on his arm. Coming from the little city of Stem, I was intrigued, and I somewhat admired the women he brought around.

I spent my off-days in Durham with my uncle instead of spending them with Wade, which started causing problems in our relationship. I did care about him and wasn't quite ready to let him go, so I invited him to spend the day with us so that he could see nothing was going on. Wade and my uncle didn't mesh well, and it became awkward. My uncle side-eyed Wade to figure out why he was getting all my time. Besides, I was his baby girl in his eyes, and he was supposed to protect me.

During the ride home, Wade berated me. "So, this is what you do all day? Sit around your uncle, inhale weed smoke, be his personal errand girl, and smile in his friend's face?" he said.

While we were there, my uncle's best friend, Bean, passed through. We hit it off, and I laughed the whole time. Wade felt intimidated, but he wasn't going to say anything in front of my uncle and his street homies.

"You're jealous, huh?" I asked.

"Hell no! Jealous of what! Some local dope boys with nothing else on their mind?" he said.

"Well, doesn't that remind you of somebody?" I couldn't believe he had just described himself.

That said, I was still on the fence regarding Wade. Until I made up my mind, I'd chill from being around my uncle and hang out with Wade to avoid confusion.

I had not returned Uncle Nino's calls in two weeks or been back home to Ma's house. I just felt like I would eventually have to choose who I would spend the majority of my time with and I was not ready to make that decision. I missed my uncle. When he was incarcerated, I prayed regularly for the day he would be clean from drugs and financially stable. My uncle grew weary because I hadn't been returning his calls and began calling Ma to question her about my relationship with Wade. My uncle thought Wade had me up under some type of spell, and he wasn't having it.

Midday, I was in there pleasing my man when I heard a knock on the door.

"Jesus! Is that the police?" I asked as I reached for my clothes on the floor.

Wade had already gone to look out the peephole to see who was banging on the door.

"It's your uncle!" he yelled.

I opened the door to find my uncle standing with his back turned to me. I shut the door behind me because I was afraid of whatever he was about to say. I didn't want Wade to be offended.

"What's going on with you, Tabitha? Your mother says you've not been home in weeks. She has no clue if you're okay or not," he said.

"First of all, I'm grown. And besides, my step dad sees me at work from time-to-time and reports back to her, so I know Ma knows I'm okay," I said as I rolled my eyes.

My uncle lectured me about how I needed to get my life together and how I was failing at an early age.

The audacity.

He punched his fist in his hand, emphasizing each point. My uncle's voice got real hoarse when he said he never wanted me to follow in his footsteps and throw my life away. I didn't understand what he meant by that, but he had valid concerns. Wade and I weren't moving forward in our lives, and the way we were humping like rabbits was eventually going to result in an ill-timed baby.

My uncle continued to interrogate me and then informed me if I didn't at least answer his calls while I was *doing me*, he'd show back up. As I watched my uncle drive away, I knew every single thing he said was true. I had some decisions to make. Was I in love with this guy, or was I in complete *lust*? I didn't see a future with him at all; we were wasting each other's time. Besides, he'd eventually leave anyway, so I'd just end it with him first.

I walked back into the house to a puppy-dog face. Wade was sure that my uncle had possibly empowered me in some way, and he wasn't happy about it. I kissed him on the forehead, packed my things, and returned to Ma's house.

At the sight of me, Ma wordlessly closed her bible and went to the kitchen to start making my favorite meal. I loved Ma so much, even though my behaviors didn't always show it. At times, I felt like she deserved a better daughter. I was all over the place and had no idea what I wanted to do with my life.

The next morning, I woke up and made a declaration to be productive. My uncle had mentioned making some money moves with him, but I didn't have a clue what that was. It had to be better than working at the pizza parlor. Ending things with Wade meant it had to be cold turkey. I didn't want to see him at all, and I wouldn't be taking his calls. That's just how I knew to function. When you make your world black and white, you make it small enough to control. And when you have power and control, you don't get hurt; you do the hurting.

The next morning, when I entered my uncle's house, he met me with a frown.

"Niece, what do you have on? It looks like you're about to go full-court press with the neighborhood dope boys," he laughed.

My uncle and his new chick-of-the-week hooted as they inhaled marijuana smoke. Now this chick was thicker than a government mule, as my uncle would say. I wasn't sure where he picked up these sayings when he referred to women, but they were hilarious to my young mind. Asia wore extensions and dressed for a night of bar hopping.

He looked at Asia and said, "I want you to take my niece out and give her a makeover. Hell, I'm tired of you wearing Jordan's, basketball shorts, and especially that ponytail."

"No thanks, Unc, I'm perfectly fine with what I have on," I said.

"Niece, if you want to make some money, I'm going to need you to look the part. Let's retire you from the parlor! You've graduated," he announced.

Eventually, I conformed and hopped in the car with Asia. Listening to her conversation on the phone made me sick to my stomach. Who talks like that?

Girl, who all gon' be there?

Oh, I know he cappin'.

I had never been around any ghetto, hood females, so I was just trying to process it all. I rode in silence. I was pondering what type of job he had for me and if it would be enough money to leave the parlor.

When we got to the mall, Asia had me try on clothes that were so tight! I could barely breathe or move. How did women do this? She piled up the clothes she liked on me and bought them. Asia told me to keep the last outfit on as we prepared to leave the mall. This chick was so hyped to impress my uncle that she was going overboard with the thoroughness. We pulled up to a hair-braiding shop twenty minutes away, and she turned to me and said, "Don't look at me like that! Get out! Lord knows you need something done to that head."

I never wanted braids. I heard sometimes these stylists braid too tight and hurt your head. She walked me into the building, told the lady what I was getting and that I needed light makeup on my face. Asia left me to fend for myself.

"You can do my hair, lady, but don't touch my face!" I said. No way was I agreeing to be a cake face.

The lady disregarded that and began braiding my hair. I sat there and held the base of each braid as she braided. An hour later, a different lady hopped on the other side of me. I'm assuming this was supposed to get me finished faster.

Hours went by, and one of the ladies that was braiding ran hot water in a container. She dipped my hair in the hot water, and a stream of steam hit my neck. Yikes! Is this what females go through to look cute? Then the lady rolled up this cart and started doing my makeup. This was, by far, the most complex experience I had ever encountered in my life. By the time I was standing up to brush the hair off me, Asia had pulled up.

"Oh my God, Niece! You are so pretty!" she said.

Wow! I've never heard anyone tell me that before. I was overlooked by everyone most of the time. I swung around and looked in the mirror. My eye filled with happy tears. I was pretty! I twirled around and even hit a two-step to showcase how excited I was. Asia and I thanked everyone that participated in my look, and we headed to her car.

Asia was so excited because she knew if she gave me the look my uncle wanted, she'd win brownie points with him. She started talking about how she and my uncle were going to get married and have babies. I tuned her out. My uncle already had two kids that he was attempting to build rapport with. He had missed out on much of their lives, and he was working to fix the mess his absence caused. Uncle Nino had spent most of his life in a jail cell; he surely wasn't going to be bound by a wife and more babies.

It was late by the time we arrived at my uncle's house. His best friend, Bean, was there. When we walked in, Bean's jaw dropped, and he said, "Wow!"

"Alright now, Bean. That's my niece, so watch yourself," my uncle said.

"I was just complimenting her, man. She's gorgeous, and you know it," Bean said as he scratched his head in complete disbelief.

I had no interest in him because he was far from my type, but I could see from multiple encounters with him how he could grow on you. No way was anything going to happen there because he had a crazy baby-mother, and nobody had time for that drama. I just wanted to get these coins my uncle was talking about and eventually save up to get my own place. I was finally in a place where I was focused and not deterred by men. So, Bean was a hard no for me.

I walked around the house, twirling and looking at it myself in every mirror that I passed by. Out of the corner of my eye, I kept catching Bean looking at me and shaking his head. I grabbed my things and headed home so that Ma could see my new look. I walked in the door, and Ma started shedding tears. Ma had always dreamed of a little girl, a little ballerina, a princess to wear dresses and all things girly, but she never got that from me. I was the one that cried and wouldn't smile for family photos because I had to wear a dress.

She said, "Oh my God, Tabitha! You look so beautiful!"

I thanked my mom and headed straight for the kitchen to see what we were having for dinner. At the dinner table, Ma played with my hair. Even though I was kind of annoyed by it, I asked her what she thought, and should I continue with this look. Ma was so proud of me for this transition. She felt as if she finally got the daughter that she longed for all these years.

Then she told me how Wade had been calling the house asking about my whereabouts. Wade had paged me several times earlier, but I ignored him. Besides, I needed to figure out what I was going to do with this relationship, and I had to decide quickly.

As I sat there in silence, Ma looked up at me and said, "If you're going to leave that boy, you need to make a decision now and tell him. You owe him an explanation, and you are not to leave him hanging. Wade is actually a good guy, Tabitha. He deserves better."

319

A part of me felt as though she was saying he deserved a better woman than me. But she was referring to how I was going about doing things. I did owe him an explanation, but I wasn't ready to give it to him. Besides, I was caught up on my new look and how I was going to maintain it. My uncle never said how I was going to make this new amount of money that he was referring to. There were so many people in my uncle's house when I got back; he told me he would talk to me the next day. At this point, I wanted the opportunity, and I didn't care what it was. Ma and pops had done the best they could do regarding raising me, and they raised me well. However, I needed something new and fascinating. Wade was falling off with his income because apparently the head guy had got knocked off, and "work" wasn't coming in as frequently as it used to. I saw a complete change in him, and I knew it was because he felt inadequate as a man. Nevertheless, I only cared about myself, and I was ready to get it.

The next morning, I called Wade and told him I had to open the pizza parlor at 9 am, and he could come by and see me if he wanted to. He was so happy to hear from me, and we made plans to do a movie night later, so we could talk and get to spend some time with each other. I started preparing the salad bar and conducting my morning prep to open the restaurant as I anticipated Wade coming by the pizza parlor to see me. I got a phone call from my uncle.

"Hey, Niece! What is going on, babe? Remember what I was telling you about the other day? Well, I'm ready for you. What time can you be over here?" he asked.

"Well, Unc, I kind of made plans to go see my boyfriend tonight, so I'm not sure today would be a good day. Maybe we can reschedule for tomorrow?" I asked.

"Niece, this isn't a regular job interview. I need you to be here today whenever you get off that job so that we can discuss these money moves!" he said.

I didn't want to let either of these men down. My temples throbbed. What was I supposed to tell Wade about our date tonight? Our very predictable date. Where we were going to watch the first ten minutes of a movie, during which Wade would complain about me spending so much time in Durham, and then we'd end up having some bomb makeup sex. The intrigue of my uncle's lifestyle, the money, and possibly seeing Bean won the day.

Three tables later, Wade appeared at the door, smiling at me. I could smell him a mile away, and boy was that red man fine.

"Hey babe," I said as I hurried to him and hugged him.

"Hey, my love. I miss you so much, and I can't wait to spend this evening with you," Wade said.

My stomach tightened when I said, "Babe about tonight, can we talk about it?"

"Yeah. Get this. My mother's giving us the house to ourselves tonight," he said.

My brain instantly went to disgust that this grown man kept wanting to dick me down in his mama's house. That had to be the worst kind of disrespect. I'd thought about my own son doing the same to me. It was wrong on so many levels.

"See, that's my point exactly. I'm tired of being stuck at your mom's house. We need our own place! And if working at this pizza parlor is our sole income, we're not going to get anywhere. Either you find a job, or I'm going to move on without you!" I blurted out before my brain caught up with my mouth.

"Babe, why are you talking to me like that? Why does your voice sound funny?" he asked.

That is something we would say amongst ourselves when we felt agitated.

"I'm sorry, babe. I'm just stressed out, and I'm tired of working at this pizza parlor. I think I have another way to make some money," I said.

"Oh? What is it? Turn me on."

"Babe, I'm not sure what it is yet until I talk to my uncle this evening. I have to cancel our movie night." I said and braced myself.

Wade's face reddened, and he left without a word. I was so livid and sick of being broke. I was sick of his nagging and complaining, but not doing anything about it. I'd been mentally checked-out of our relationship for a while. It was really over as far as I was concerned.

After work, I hurried home and sorted through my new clothes, and I picked out the tightest jeans. My uncle's homeboys would be checking for me, and I had to be cute. I pulled up at my uncle's house around 7 pm. I entered the basement thick with marijuana smoke where people played video games, gambling, and smoked. I sat there for a while, waiting until my uncle was free. Bean pulled up in a little swatter that my uncle gave him to drive to maintain a *low profile and deter the stick-up kids.* I still wondered why he drove that car, especially if he was making all this money my uncle spoke of.

I let Bean in and returned to the couch only to realize he continued to stare at me.

"What's up, Bean? How are you?" I asked.

"I'm better now," he said with a smirk.

There was something about him that I could not put my finger on. He wasn't the cutest, but his sense of humor, his swag, and persistence were captivating.

My uncle looked over at me and said, "Niece, I need you to drive Bean somewhere."

Bean and I headed for the door. I wasn't sure where we were going or what we were doing. I just knew the outcome was going to be income. As soon as we got in the car, my pager pulsed with pages from Wade.

"You still got a pager, baby girl? We need to get you a cellphone!" he said.

"I know, but I'm in no position to buy one now," I replied.

"Who that paging you? Your little boyfriend that was with you last time?" he asked.

I side-eyed him and didn't respond.

"Where to?" I asked.

"Go to the top of the hill and make the left. And put your seatbelt on and get comfortable, we have an hour drive ahead of us," he said.

Bean recited directions and merged onto the highway. Bean tried to mask the extended moments of awkward silence by playing with the radio and rolling the window up and down for no apparent reason.

Our destination was a secluded area. Three guys in a car pulled up beside us. Bean hopped out of the car and got in the backseat of the mysterious car. A beat later, Bean exited, popped his trunk, and got back into the car with me.

"Drive," he said.

I kept my mouth shut and drove. We engaged in more conversation on the way back.

"What's your story?" he asked.

"Why are you so nosy?" I asked.

"You're just interesting, that's all. Is there anything wrong with that?"

He directed me to pull over to the side of the road.

"What's wrong? Is something wrong with the car? Do we have a flat tire?" I asked

"No, I told you to pull over because I want you," he said.

Bean reached out and pulled my face towards his and kissed me deep and hard. No one had ever been that aggressive with me before, and it turned me on. The next thing I knew, we were in the backseat butt-naked, and he was inside me. Now, other guys I had sex with may have been larger, but this was passionate lovemaking, and it took me to another level. The spontaneity was exciting, and I was enjoying every single moment of it. Afterward, Bean stroked my face and gazed at me.

"What's that about?" I asked.

"You know that was exactly what you wanted," he said.

I turned away from him to dress. The thought of being caught or someone watching us was intriguing. Bean's pager rumbled with back-to-back pages. It was either Uncle Nino or Bean's ghetto baby-mother.

"We have to get back," I said.

"I know. Nino is going to be looking for us," he replied.

When we arrived at Uncle Nino's, he was pissed, "What happened? You two got lost?"

"No, sir, I wasn't feeling well, so we had to pull over at a store. I think it probably was something I ate," I replied, staring at my feet.

I was very much aware that in trying to be all things to all people and in navigating the adult world, I'd turned into a compulsive liar. But I wasn't comfortable being in the thick of a lie. I felt dirty, on edge, and wanted to get out of there.

"Uncle Nino, can I go now? It's getting late, and I know Ma is going to be looking for me."

Uncle Nino nodded in the direction of the bedroom, so I followed him. He pulled three crisps one-hundred-dollar bills out of a safe and handed them me.

"What's this for?" I asked.

"For the job you completed tonight!" he said.

"But I didn't do anything but drive Bean."

"And that will be your job moving forward. I need you to look pretty, keep yourself up, and drive," he said.

"That's it? And I keep this amount of money every time?" I asked.

"Sometimes it will be more. Sometimes it will be less. It just all depends on *the job*." He winked and walked back into the living room to play his video games.

I couldn't believe it. What I made in three hours was two weeks' worth of busting my ass and dealing with the public at the pizza parlor. If this were consistent, I'd quit the pizza parlor and work for Uncle Nino full-time. No more getting dirty, smelling like food, dealing with rude customers, and working for chump change. Boy, was I onto something!

It was super-late by the time I got home, so I was extra-quiet. I thought Ma was psychic. She would speak on specific outcomes that would come to pass. For example, I recollect her telling Uncle Nino before he was incarcerated the last time about a dream she had about him. She told him that she saw a police raid at his home and he was being taken out in handcuffs. This dream came to pass four days later.

Although being arrested for illegal activity, never really crossed my mind, maybe it was a possibility. Then, my thoughts drifted back to the quick revenue I could generate making *runs* and I couldn't handle much more. Not tonight.

Moments later, Ma appeared in my doorway.

"It's late," she said.

"I know. What time it is, Ma. I was with Uncle Nino, and I lost track of time. Besides, if you had not noticed yet, I'm kind of grown," I said.

"You're going to find out just how grown you are if you come to my house again this late," she said and shut my door.

I was so over being controlled, and I had to figure out a way to get my own place.

The next morning, I woke to a 6 am page from Uncle Nino.

I looked for the house phone to call him.

"Tabitha, I need you to meet Bean for a run at 8 am. Can you be here?" he asked.

"Yes sir, I'll be there," I replied.

I hung up, still processing what happened last night with Wade, and then Bean, and then... the money! I left the house an hour later and broke all the speed limits the whole way to Durham to get there on time. This drive normally took forty-five minutes, but I completed it right at the thirty minute mark. That was another reason I wanted my own place. My life was due for major changes, and one of them would be Wade. He was in my way.

I was surprised to see Bean and Uncle Nino smoking marijuana in the living room and playing video games this early in the day. I was slightly irritated that I raced over here only to have to sit and watch Uncle Nino finish his video game.

Uncle Nino said that I needed a cellphone and to plan on crashing with him a few nights a week so that I would be closer. I was excited about getting a cellphone, and could finally be done with that pager. He didn't have any "serious" work for me right then but tasked me with a list of errands.

I was excited as I bought a Blackberry, which was *the* phone to have. As soon as it was activated, I called my friend Natalie, one of my former teammates who I knew since moving to Butner. Natalie was a particularly good friend, having educated me on my cycle, how to insert tampons, and she introduced me to getting my unibrow waxed.

"Hey, girl, what's up? Remember, you were talking about moving to Durham?" I asked.

"Yes, I found an apartment I like. I'm afraid I won't be able to afford it, though," she said.

Natalie graduated from high school and got a job at one of the banks in Durham. But she was experiencing the same struggles living at home with her parents. She was ready to be on her own. Nobody I knew wanted to go to college. The only reason I would have gone to college was by way of a GSU basketball scholarship. That possibility was a tiny dot in my rearview mirror.

"So, what if I told you I have two jobs now, and could actually help you split the bills?" I asked.

"What! Are you serious, Tabitha? I'm about to cry tears of joy! You have no idea how bad I need to get away from them," she said, referring to the parental units.

Natalie and I discussed the move, and we decided to sign the lease for the first of the month, which was days away. I didn't have any money saved at all.

After running Uncle Nino's errands, I went home, called him to give him my new number, and told him to pass it on to Bean for business purposes.

I jumped out of the shower, and my Blackberry rang.

"Tabitha. This is Bean. Get dressed and come out," he said.

"Are you kidding me? My mother is going to kick me out if I stay out until the wee hours of the morning."

"I'll get you a room. You don't have to go back tonight. Meet me at the Doubletree off Highway 55 in an hour," he said.

Bean hung up. He did not even wait for me to answer, which meant he was confident enough to assume I was coming. I liked that. His assertiveness and self-confidence got my adrenaline flowing.

I got dressed and peeked out into the living room to see Ma engaged in her nightly routine of reading the bible. I crept down the hall, and when I reached the backdoor, I sprayed the hinges with oil sheen. I opened the door and ran to my car. When I backed out of the driveway, I didn't cut my lights on until I was halfway up the street.

Did I really like this guy? What was happening?

I pulled up at this nice, huge hotel an hour later and called Bean for the room number. I rushed through the lobby and up to the fourth floor. My knuckles just made contact with the door, when Bean ripped it open with a smile on his face. Without a word, he kissed me and pulled me into the room. After intense foreplay, he had me on my stomach, attempting to reclaim his time. I enjoyed my ability to drive him crazy. I was quickly discovering the power of sex.

We laid in each other's arms for hours, talking about life and how unhappy he was with his son's mother.

"Why don't you just leave?" I asked.

Bean explained it wasn't that simple. If he was going to be out of the house for good, he was concerned about her having not one, but multiple men around their son.

"You just can't live your life like that. Why remain miserable in a situation because you have a child with someone?" I asked. Obviously, I wasn't talking from experience, but I felt convicted living in a distressed home was worse than divorce for kids.

"You're talking about me. What happened to the guy you were dating?" he asked.

I cringed at the thought that I had not closed that door with Wade yet. Ma told me he'd been calling the house and coming by. He was in tears because of my detached and nonchalant behavior and didn't understand how I could just wake up and decide not to be with him anymore. I thought I loved Wade, but it wasn't love, and *that* wasn't my fault.

The next morning, I did the walk of shame back to the house around noon after laying up with Bean all night. Thank God the house was empty, so I showered and prepared for my phone call with Wade.

"Hello. How have you been?" I asked.

Wade didn't respond.

"This isn't working for me anymore, and I don't want to keep wasting your time," I said.

"Is there someone else?" Wade said.

I assured him I wasn't seeing anyone else, but I was transitioning to more independence by getting my own place in Durham, improving myself, and moving on. Wade pushed back on everything I said, so I wished him well, and I ended the call.

The next day, Natalie and I signed a lease and moved into our apartment. Two days later, the hospital Ma worked at called to offer me a unit secretary position I'd applied for. I accepted the job and put my notice in at the pizza parlor. I was shutting the door on life in Butner and its attachments.

In the meantime, Bean and I still messed around when he wasn't schooling me about the pickups I was engaged in. I knew these pickups had to be something illegal; I just wasn't quite sure what it was. I was operating under the umbrella of delusional invincibility, so I continued with the pickups and my new job at the hospital. I only worked at the hospital three days a week on the night shift, so I had a lot of free time.

Because of all my hard work, Uncle Nino had purchased me a new Acura Integra and had rimmed it up. He called me one day and asked me to take him to a Jamaican restaurant. Uncle Nino liked to be chauffeured around since he felt as though he had reached *boss* status.

"I'm on my way Uncle Nino," I assured him.

When we got there, Uncle Nino hopped out of the car and greeted this beautiful Jamaican man. They shook hands and talked for thirty minutes before approaching my car. The Jamaican looked paranoid because my windows were smoked out with tint, so he probably wanted to make sure my uncle wasn't on any foolery.

Uncle Nino introduced me to Sly. My hands were damp with sweat before I reached out the window to greet him.

"Well, hello there, beautiful girl," he said in his lilting accent. Sly held on to my hand and kissed it.

The word "beautiful" was being thrown my way more and more as the days went by, and I liked it. Our eyes locked, and then Uncle Nino asked if I was hungry. I was catching on with how street life worked. Sly was at the top of this food pyramid.

I surely needed him on my team. Maybe I could throw him some of this good coochie or make him wait for it and let him spend all his money on me like Bean was starting to do. Based on Sly's jewels, his money was way longer than Uncle Nino's and Bean's put together.

Uncle Nino and I sat down and ate some of the best Jamaican food I'd ever had in my entire life. We discussed my goals and getting my life together. He asked me what I wanted to do with my life, and at the age of twenty, I had no idea. Uncle Nino was becoming more of a father figure to me now since he'd consistently been home from his last incarceration. My step dad and my mother did the best they could raising all of us; however, I still always craved fatherly love. At times, I chased it in the men that I dealt with.

On the way home, Uncle Nino said that I would be meeting with Sly twice a week, moving forward. Bean and I would no longer be doing pickups. He explained that Bean was his best friend, and sometimes you can't do business with friends. Uncle Nino reiterated that there wasn't any bad blood, but this adjustment would help Bean get ahead. I was perfectly fine with that and looked forward to seeing more of Sly every week.

The following week, I moved into my place with Natalie. Things were great until Bean came over, which would seemingly send Natalie into a tailspin. She would slam doors, throw things around, and just looked miserable when he was there. At first, I thought I imagined things until Bean noticed it as well. Natalie's behavior really wasn't top of mind. I gave Bean an ultimatum: I was going to stop dealing with him if he was going to remain in the house with his son's mother. The next day, he phoned me to inform me that he was in love with me and that he left.

"Left to go where?" I asked.

"I left her. I packed all of my things up and left," he said.

"So, where are you going to live now?" I asked.

Bean couldn't come stay with me because Natalie could barely tolerate him just visiting.

"I'm back at my mom's house, for now," he said.

Conveniently enough, his mother stayed eight minutes away from my apartment. But the more Bean came over, the more peculiar Natalie got.

After Bean left one day, I finally asked, "What's your problem?"

She became quiet and didn't respond to anything I said. We'd been living together for less than a month.

"I'm in love with you! Can't you see that?" she yelled. "I thought that's why you wanted to move together. I thought that you had these same feelings! But all you want to do is be laid up under some dick, and I'm sick of it!" she cried.

Whoa! That caught me totally by surprise! I had no idea Natalie liked women.

I mean, we were all tomboys, and we played sports together. Never did I judge anyone who liked the same sex; however, I had never been exposed to it directly. It wasn't something that I could see myself indulging in. I respected how she felt; I just could not be a part of it. I wanted out of this apartment, but we had just signed the lease. There was no way I could ever be comfortable bringing my company to our home with me knowing that she was feeling me. *Literally.*

I went to the leasing office the next day and discussed my options with one of the rental agents. Unfortunately, Natalie's signature was required to get out of the lease without being sued by her for monies owed towards future rent. When things like this started transpiring, I wondered if this was my karma for the way I mistreated Wade recently. But I was moving on to what seemed to be a better life.

Later, that day I had to meet Sly for one of our weekly visits, and he seemed concerned because I wasn't my usual ebullient self.

"What's wrong with you, pretty lady?" he asked.

Boy did I love his accent.

I told him about my situation with Natalie, how I was trying to get out of the lease, and attempting to figure out what my next moves were.

"That's really simple. All you have to do now is just get your own place," he said.

"How am I supposed to do that when I don't have any credit? I could never get anything in my name," I said.

"Be careful with your words, Love. The universe is listening," he said. "Baby girl, as long as you got money, you can finesse the credit portion of whatever you're applying for. How much are you in need to actually move into your own place?" he asked.

"I don't even know where to start," I sighed.

Sly excused himself and disappeared into the restaurant for ten minutes. When he came back out, he dumped a blue sack on my lap and said, "I wish I had your problems."

"Don't open this until you actually go to apply for your apartment. Also, tell your uncle I said hello, and I'll call him later," Sly said.

I drove away from Sly and before I even turned the corner, I ripped open the blue sack. The anticipation from what was possibly in it was killing me. As I opened the sack, hundreds of dollars fell out into my lap. I begin to count and count and count. After I got to a little over two thousand dollars, I was interrupted by a car blowing the horn at me to proceed through the traffic light. I pulled over to the side of the road and wondered what I did to deserve this amount of money from a man I'd never been intimate with.

The money added up to five-thousand-dollars. I wanted to cry, but anxiety consumed me. This was all contingent on Natalie signing the lease to free me from any liability.

As I was driving back from Sly's restaurant, I spotted a big sign that said, "Brand New Luxury Apartment Homes: Now Leasing." I turned off and drove through this scenic community, not even ten minutes from Sly's restaurant. The landscaping was stunning alongside a wooded area, and the buildings were made from an attractive grey rock material. I pulled up to the leasing office and sat in my car for a second. I think it was time I had a talk with this God my mother spoke of.

"Okay God, are you there? I need you on this one," I said. I didn't know how this worked. Do I wait for a response? Or do I just walk in there knowing God has my back? When I walked into the leasing office, I was greeted by a pleasant, attentive young lady.

"Welcome home. Would you like to get moved into one of our beautiful apartment homes today?" she asked.

"Sure. Do you guys have anything for immediate move in? I have the money now," I said.

She laughed and said, "Well, that's a plus, but let me show you a unit first."

I walked into a third-floor unit and instantly fell in love. It was way nicer than the place Natalie and I had. It had vaulted ceilings, granite countertops, a garden tub, and a plethora of other amazing amenities.

"How do you like it?" she said.

"I love it! Where do I sign?" I asked.

I started filling out the paperwork and prayed that Natalie would sign to have me taken off the lease. The leasing agent told me I was approved with one month's rent deposit. I pulled out five-hundred-dollars from my sack and handed it to her.

I left with the keys and went to find Natalie to tell her the news.

She was laid up with one of our local friends on the couch, someone I knew from hanging around the boys in Uncle Nino's hood. So much for wanting to be with me!

"Natalie, can I speak to you for a minute? In private?"

"You can say whatever you need to say to me in front of him," she said.

"Okay, cool. I need you to sign the lease, so I can get out of here. I already found a new place and signed the lease, and I'm moving tonight," I said.

"No way! You're liable for this place as well," she yelled, being extra dramatic for her friend.

Before I had to blacken my childhood friends' eye, I just left. I was so pissed and needed to vent, so I called Bean. His solution was to get me a room until I figured it out.

"No thank you, I'm just going to grab an air mattress for the night and head to my new place," I said.

Bean was a little caught off-guard when I mentioned I already had a new place, but the excitement in his voice at the thought of me having my own place gave me so much peace. I knew he was struggling to make it, so he wouldn't have to stand on the corner anymore after parting ways with my uncle. He definitely would not be much help with my bills. But I had a feeling Sly had a crush on me, so I knew if I needed anything, he had me.

Bean said he could meet me to get whatever I needed to be comfortable. It was a relief that he had my back.

When we got to the new apartment, Bean tossed my things on the floor and said, "Where did this money come from in this blue sack?" of my empty apartment.

I wasn't prepared for that question.

"I-I-I have that money from my paychecks from work and the money from my "runs." Why do you ask me that?" I said nervously.

"It's just not safe for you to walk around with that type of cash. Why don't you put it in the bank?" he asked.

"Well, I don't have a banking account. Do I need one?" I asked.

"Of course, Tabitha. We will open one first thing in the morning," he replied.

Bean blew the air mattress up, and as soon it was nice and firm, he started to undress me. It felt so good making love to him in the comfort of my own home and not having to keep my moaning volume to a minimum.

I had to work the next morning, so I dropped by super-early at the old place to shower and change clothes. While I was showering, Natalie appeared in the doorway.

"I'm going to do it. I'll sign for you to get out of the lease," she said.

"Thank you," is all I said as I turned off the shower and rushed for work.

With Bean's help, I finally got settled into my place. Once I told Sly about finding a place, he asked me to meet him there. He walked into my empty place and shook his head in disbelief.

"No, no, no, my baby. You don't have a ting in here," he said.

"I know. I just have to work harder," I told him.

"No worries, my baby. Let me place a few calls to dem in the morning for you," Sly said.

There were times I barely understood what he said, but I know that meant he was taking care of my furniture needs. Sly was amazing! I could not even tell anyone the good news outside of my mother. Ma and I became closer regarding talking on the phone every day since I moved out. Maybe that is what we needed. Before I left, there was so much tension, and I wanted to rectify that.

I told her about the good news, who my sponsor was, and begged her not to say anything. Ma knew of Sly from my uncle, but she didn't know him personally. She promised she would not speak a word to him about it. Besides, Uncle Nino would be livid if he knew I was kicking it with his best friend and "the plug" (supplier).

I felt like things were on the right track. Sly arranged so that I could go to the furniture store and pick out whatever furniture I wanted at no expense to me. I set everything up to be delivered and left to make my normal "runs" for Uncle Nino.

In the next couple of weeks, I found myself spending more time with Sly than Bean, and Bean was starting to notice. Bean was cool, but Sly had more money. My girls from back home were hitting me up to go to Myrtle Beach for the Bike Fest. I wasn't sure what that was and had never traveled anywhere, so I was curious. Bike Fest was a weekend full of fit men on motorcycles and tons of fun. I was down, so we booked a hotel on the strip and had Sly rent us a brand-new SUV for traveling. Life was good at this point, and I was starting to see the fruits of my labor. I had been working both jobs and juggling my men. Even though the situation reeked of deceit, I was free, and that was all that mattered.

Before we hit the highway, I wanted to stop by Sly's restaurant and thank him for everything. Sly had not pressured me to sleep with him; he just wanted to see me happy. He invited all of us in for lunch to make sure we ate before we got on the road. He was so considerate and loving. I introduced him to all my friends, and we got the royal treatment.

As we left the restaurant, I handed my girls the keys to the car so that I could talk to Sly alone for a few minutes. Sly handed me another blue sack, and I twirled it around as I listened to the latest issues with his baby-mama. Apparently, the baby-mama had been sleeping around with an NFL player in Charlotte, North Carolina who was found hiding in a trunk and arrested for the murder of his pregnant girlfriend. Sly was angry that his daughter was possibly exposed to this murderer.

Sly was tall, so I reached up to rub his head and give him some comfort. He liked to play like I did, so he lifted me in the air, and as he brought me back down, he kissed me in my mouth. I wasn't sexually attracted to Sly at all. I did the bare minimum to keep him happy. Uncle Nino used to talk about all the women Sly had, but that didn't bother me. Let them other women do strange things with him, and in the interim, I'd be happy to reap the benefits.

As we got on the highway with the music blasting and we were singing all the latest hits, my phone rang.

"So, when were you going to tell me that your hoe ass was messing with the plug?" "Bean, what are you talking about?" I asked.

"I just saw you with him! Kissing him in the mouth! Is this what we're doing? I left my son's mother for you!" he cried.

Apparently, Bean was outside of the restaurant with his homeboys in the car when I was leaving the restaurant. He explained that it was embarrassing as a man. Bean said that he always spoke so highly of me, but I was just another one of his hoes.

"First of all, no one asked you to leave her! You said you were unhappy and left on your own! And hoe? Who are you calling a hoe?"

My friend snatched the phone from me, hung up, and said, "We are not about to do this on our vacation. The hell with him! Plus, you said the dick isn't that big anyways."

She had a valid point as they all chimed in. They reminded me that I still had Sly, so why was I sweating Bean's broke-ass?

"He's not broke, you all, he's getting back on his feet," I said in his defense.

I cranked the music up and acted as if I didn't care. But I wondered about how long Bean would be mad. Even though Sly kicked out the most money, Bean had more time to spend with me. I required a lot of attention, and that is what he gave me. But we were not really *together*. These men and their double-standards never seemed to amaze me.

We arrived at the beach, and my girls were ready for whatever. We were all borderline single, and I was feeling their energy. We agreed that what happens in Myrtle Beach, stays in Myrtle Beach. When we got to the hotel, we changed our traveling clothes into the skimpiest clothes we could find. We hit the strip and walked until our feet hurt.

This was unknown territory for me, but my girls had been before, so I was following their leads. We hopped on and off motorcycles and hung out with guys all night long. One set of guys from Virginia had a condo off the strip. We went back with them, grilled out, and partied hard. The liquor flowed, the clothes came off, and anything you can imagine went on in that house. The guy I was with was a little more reserved and if I wanted to take a walk on the beach.

I welcomed the escape. And it didn't hurt that he was well-muscled and handsome. But he stood apart from the others, just seemed more settled and mature. I wanted to turn up with my girls, but at that moment, he needed someone to talk to, so I listened. William was six years older than me and talked about getting married one day and having kids.

Not with me!

"How old are you, if you don't mind me asking?" he said.

"I'm only nineteen, and kids are at the bottom of my list. I don't want any kids. What would I do with another human that I'm responsible for?"

William got quiet and frowned.

By the time we got back in the house, my girls were all drunk and dancing provocatively. Even though I was down for the cause, I was too shy for that with complete strangers. William and I grabbed some drinks, copped a squat in the corner, and laughed at everyone the rest of the night.

William asked if I wanted to go back to the strip or spend the night with him. I wanted to sleep with him so bad; I opted to stay there.

I was in fling-mode, so I wanted to get this over with and get back to all the chaos I had going on at home. Bean had not called back.

William started taking my clothes off when he got to his room. Then my phone rang.

"I'm here. Where are you?" Sly said.

The three-thousand-dollars in the blue bag flashed in my mind.

"I'm with the girls at a beach house off the strip," I said.

"You're over there with guys, aren't you?" he asked.

"Does it matter? We're not together, Sly!" I yelled.

What the hell? Was this a conspiracy?

I hung up.

"Trouble in paradise? I thought you said you were single," William said.

Ugh. Now he was questioning me too. I turned around and looked at William, now naked, and substantially endowed. Any thoughts of Sly or Bean dissolved. I ran over to William and took on the challenge of his huge penis.

That sex session lasted for hours, and by the time we were done, I could barely walk. William was cuddled up asleep when my girls called me from downstairs. I was too exhausted to move. I texted them to leave without me. Ma would not be happy. She always said, "If you come together, leave together."

The next morning, I woke up to a dry phone. Usually, Bean or Sly would have called or texted, but there was nothing. I was going to clean this up when I got back; they weren't going anywhere. We finished out our weekend with a bang, managing to stay stuck up under the Virginia crew for the duration. When it was time to get back home, William and I exchanged numbers and promised to keep in touch. But that was unlikely.

Chapter 15: It Ain't Safe

An hour into the drive back home from the beach, I called Bean and asked him to meet me at my place. I hid a key over the top of the door and told him to use it to get in if he beat me there. I dropped all the girls off at their cars and headed home. When I pulled up to my apartment, Bean's car was already there. I left my luggage in the car in hopes that he would get it for me.

I opened the door and walked into him, lying across the couch watching television.

"Hi there," I said.

I'd never seen Bean look so somber before. I sat on his lap, and he promptly pushed me off.

"Are you serious? How long are you going to be mad?" I asked.

"Tabitha, how long have you been dealing with Jamaican Sly?" he asked.

"It depends on what you mean by *dealing with*. I never slept with him if that's your concern," I said.

"Well, who else have you been sleeping with? Anyone at the beach?" he asked as he continued to watch the television.

"Look, if you're not going to trust me, why are you around?" I asked.

Bean went into a series of questions about Sly and expected me to answer them. I told him Sly was giving me money and that I liked him. But, I saw myself with him in the future.

"I'm young and just having fun now. You should understand that," I said.

Bean was older than me, focused on getting his money up to become his own boss eventually; he was more settled than me. But he was still staying with his mother and had not sat me down to discuss being serious yet, so I was playing the field.

Just then, I heard a noise in my bedroom.

Sly emerged from the bedroom. He took a seat across from us, sitting on the furniture he had purchased.

"At this point, you're going to have to decide who you want to be with—no more straddling the fence. We do business together, and this is starting to affect our relationship. So, you choose now!" he said sternly.

I was so pissed that they were even discussing me. So, Sly had come to the beach to confront me, but I dodged him. This man had spent thousands of dollars on me, but we were not exclusively dating or having sex. I still didn't see what the problem was and why I couldn't have both of them.

I thought about who I wanted to keep around. Sly had baby-mama drama, seeing multiple women, and he was super-controlling. Bean had a lot of time for me, probably because he wasn't busy making money.

"If I must decide, I choose to continue what I have with Bean," I said calmly as I looked Sly in the face.

"Then, it is settled. Don't call me for anything else, and I wish you two the best," Sly said, as he left the apartment.

What did this mean for Bean and Sly's relationship? I had made a grave mistake. "Welp, there goes my plug. I guess I'll have to link back with your uncle," Bean said.

But Uncle Nino didn't know that I was sleeping with *the help*.

"Because of you, this has set me back tremendously. But I love you, and I'm willing to do whatever it takes to provide for you. I don't have the type of money Sly has, but if you stick with me, I *will* get there," he said.

"Babe, did you just say you loved me?" I asked.

He responded quickly, "Yes, Tabitha, I love you! I'd do anything for you!"

That made things totally different now. He knew all that I had done, and he still loved me. I was sold on being with him exclusively. Screw what Uncle Nino thought and forget the money; we would figure it out.

Over the next couple of months, things got worse. Someone told Uncle Nino that Bean and I were together, so he confronted us. We told him the truth, and he stopped talking to us for weeks on end. I couldn't understand why he was so mad. Maybe Uncle Nino was trying to protect me – I don't know. Nevertheless, I was happy, and I was going to stay with Bean.

Things were also bad at my hospital job. I'd been late frequently and called out a few times in the last couple of months, so I was placed on probation. I was so consumed with doing things for my uncle and living the fast life, that work not a priority. However, I needed my job more than ever because Bean prohibited me for doing runs for Uncle Nino and banned me from seeing Sly.

At the hospital, I was called to the office and warned not to be late or miss another day for the next six months. I signed an agreement regarding the repercussions associated with my actions. I rotated twelve-hour morning and night shifts and must have misread the schedule. Subsequently, one morning, I awoke to three missed calls from work. I arrived an hour late despite rushing and driving like a maniac. I was thirty minutes into my shift when my manager called me into her office. She terminated me on the spot.

What was I going to do?

Bean was living with me now, but he was trying to flip his money and get back on his feet in the middle of a drought. My rent was due, so I wrote a bad check hoping it would just clear, and I could take care of the overdrawn charges later. I hadn't told Bean about losing my job. I thought I'd downplay the hospital job and find another gig.

I'd leave the apartment when I was supposed to work and go somewhere to kill time. I didn't want anyone to think I was a failure. That meant I had nobody to turn to, and even had to resist a strong urge to call Sly.

Soon enough, my check bounced, and I had an eviction notice. Bean walked in the house with the letter in his hand, asking what it was, and I just broke down crying. I finally had the guts to tell him I'd been lying the whole time and what a mess I'd made. Bean kneeled on the floor to hold me as I cried like a newborn baby.

Bean was quiet for a while, and then he assured me that he would take care of everything. I had my doubts because I knew his financial situation.

The next day, Bean cleared the balance for the leasing office, so I had a little bit more relief. I still needed to find a job, and that was what I started to seek since everything was out in the open now. Bean continued to leave every morning to stand on the block, and I would sleep in. He doubled-back one morning and realized that all I had been doing was sleeping. I woke up to a splash of cold water in my face.

As I gasped for air, he yelled, "Get your ass up, Tabitha! You can't sleep your life away!"

I dried myself off and went to sit in the living room with Bean.

"You don't have a high school diploma, right?" he asked.

"No, I don't, and you know it." My response was laced with sarcasm.

"I want you to go back to school and get your high school diploma. Once that's complete, you get a trade, so you can make yourself more marketable. You're a smart girl, but you have to get busy," Bean said.

I nodded. I always did great in school, but I just followed the wrong path, thinking that I was getting ahead by working and making money. The reality is I was getting nowhere, and I was mentally stagnated.

The next morning, Bean took me to the local community college to get signed up. It was an awkward experience to have him by my side. But I enjoyed the time we spent together because it was rare nowadays. Now that he was earning more, I was already asleep before he even got home. I signed up, and classes started a month later. While I sat at home and waited for classes to start, Bean had me doing tasks to help him speed up his sales. That got old fast.

Classes started, and it felt strange sitting in a classroom full of adults who also hadn't attained this milestone. This was the only way I could maintain being a dope-boy's wifey. The first day, I met this girl named Tia in class, and we discussed life outside of class. The class wasn't structured. You studied on your own and then tested on that subject. Tia informed me there was the general equivalency testing option as well. Instead of taking one subject at a time and attending for a year, I could use class time to brush up on everything with the resources provided and then test out of the program. GED had my name written all over it.

After class, Tia and I would eat and hang out. We had a lot in common, even down to our boyfriend's occupations, so we just clicked. We also started going to local clubs and partying. Bean was getting impatient with my increasing absences from home and finally asked who this Tia person was. So, I invited Tia over for dinner one night, so he could get to know her. We laughed and engaged in our normal routine, but Bean was very standoffish.

"I don't like her! Something's fishy about her. I just can't put my finger on it," he said.

I brushed him off and continued to talk to my new friend. Tia was impressively popular in the Durham area; she knew everybody. That worked for me because I was trying to get in the mix and meet new people, and she was that portal for me. Since Bean went from shit to sugar overnight, I became known as "Bean's girlfriend." I thought this was cute at the time. He was making real money now and even had people working for him. With Bean's elevated status, I became high maintenance. I was getting my hair braided every two weeks, and that was costing me two-hundred-and-fifty bucks a pop. I was out shopping every day with Tia when she was off of her part-time job.

After three weeks, I was tired of school, so I requested to test out. My instructor thought I was insane because she was convinced that I hadn't had enough review yet. My attention span just was not long enough to be sitting still for three hours at a time. My instructor agreed to let me test out early, although she wanted us to commit to eight weeks before testing.

"I have never done this before, but it's just something about you that's making me go against my policy in this course," she said as I left to study for my test the next day.

I wasn't exactly enthused about this GED business, but my instructor was passionate about it, so I was always energetic when I spoke to her. I shut my phone down from the world and spent the entire night studying.

The next morning, I was escorted to an isolated area so that I could take my test. I was expecting some heightened anxiety because I did not want to fail this test. The material entailed the basics and was similar to middle school curriculum if I had to depict it. Maybe it was just because I easily retained information and Ma would always praise me for being so smart. After two hours, I completed my last question when the beeper went off.

When I got home, I looked for Bean because this day marked the tenth anniversary of his brother's death. His brother had been shot in a failed attempted burglary of a home ten years before we started dating. I called Bean's phone for four hours straight, but his phone continued to ring. The whole day passed by without a word from Bean. I got worried and started to place phone calls. That was not in his character to get missing, so I thought something must have happened. I started calling all the jails and inquiring about him. And then I called Uncle Nino.

"Uncle Nino, have you heard from Bean? I'm worried because he's not returning my calls, "I asked politely.

"Tabitha, I haven't heard from Bean at all. Nor have I seen him today. Is everything okay?" he asked.

At this point, I was under the assumption that he was trying to be nosey, so I governed myself accordingly.

"Yes, sir. It's just that today is the anniversary of his brother's death, and he won't return my calls. I'm so worried Uncle Nino," I said.

"This happens every year around this time, Tabitha. Just give him some time to himself and let him come around. He worships the ground you walk on, so I'm sure he'll come home soon," he said.

Uncle Nino and I didn't make peace on that call, but the concern and the softening of his sharp edges let me know he was coming around.

"You're right Uncle Nino, I'll wait up for him," I said.

I dozed off on the couch. When I woke up, Bean was still nowhere in sight. I got in the car and went to search for him. I rode through the Southside and then by his mother's house. A few minutes later, I got a phone call from Bean.

"Are you at a party? Are you with that girl?" he yelled.

I was trying to give him some grace since this day was touchy for him.

Gently, I said, "No. Bean, what are you talking about? I've been looking for you for hours and calling you all day, and I haven't heard from you."

"Oh, don't worry about me now," he said and hung up.

When I arrived home, Bean was sitting in the living room. Something in the air wasn't right, but I was just so relieved to see him in one piece. Bean jumped up and started pacing back-and-forth. I approached him for a hug, but he responded by punching me in the face.

I was stunned. Wait. Was this an accident where I ran up on him and scared him? Blood gushed from my bottom lip.

"Why? Why did you hit me?" You *cannot* hit me! Why did you just put your hands on me?" I cried.

Bean smacked me in the face, which knocked me to the ground. All I could do was cry because I was unsure as to why he was putting his hands on me. I started to experience a range of emotions from fear to anger to rage. I cherished Bean so much that I opted to be in a relationship with him over my *cash cow,* and this was the *thanks* I was getting? I felt more like a bad person than a victim within this moment because this was starting to become a cycle in regard to the men in my life.

Abuse was my portion.

I could not believe this was happening again.

I hadn't been physically assaulted since Korey G. put his hands on me back in the day, but I thought those days were over. There were no signs of Bean being abusive. None. I was bewildered.

"Are you okay? I'm sorry. I don't know what came over me," he said and dropped down to his knees, attempting to console me.

"No! Get away from me!" I said.

"I'm sorry, babe, I'm sorry! I just got a lot of my mind, and today is his anniversary! I'm sorry, and I wasn't supposed to hit you," he said.

At this point, I just laid on the floor, and a myriad of thoughts ran through my head.

I overheard a conversation in the hood one day that Bean indeed put his hands on women. One time, Bean fought with his baby-mother in the middle of the street. I brushed off the rumors and attributed them to people just not wanting us to be happy together. I also thought Bean would never lay a hand on me because he loved me so much. I thought I was different.

That was the day I should have grabbed Bean's belongings, thrown them on the sidewalk, and walked away from the relationship. But I was entirely dependent on him, so I stayed. The next morning, I woke up to a swollen lip, and it looked as if I had been stung by a bee. My face was all messed up. I used to watch things like this on television, and now I was at the hands of an abuser. *Again.* He promised me that he would not do it again and told me he would take me shopping the next day for all my favorite things.

What was I going to do?

I couldn't go around my family and friends with these marks on my face. Tia called me the next morning to ask me to go to lunch, and I declined.

"Girl, what's up with you? Why you don't want to go out?" she asked.

Tia knew I had become the social butterfly since being around her, and she knew I loved the attention. I never got this much attention from anyone, so I craved it.

"Girl, I'm just tired. Bean and I are having some issues, so I'd just rather be at home when he gets here," I said

Tia busted out laughing and said, "Well, okay then housewife, no worries. I'll just stop by and see you later."

"No! We have things planned, so please don't stop by. I'll just get up with you later," I said and hung up the phone abruptly.

It was not normal for Tia to say she'd drop by later, so she was picking up that something was going on. I was still trying to process everything in my head.

Was this just a onetime ordeal? Or was the physical abuse going to get worse?

Bean was my man, and he needed me, so I was going to stick it out.

What kind of woman would I be if I left him?